RENOVATE

your

RELATIONSHIPS

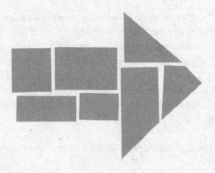

RENOVATE
your
RELATIONSHIPS

A PROVEN GUIDE TO SETTING
BOUNDARIES AND BUILDING BRIDGES
with THOSE WHO MATTER MOST

SCOTT VAUDREY, MD, MA

NELSON
BOOKS

An Imprint of Thomas Nelson

Published in Nashville, Tennessee, by Nelson Books, an imprint of Thomas Nelson. Nelson Books and Thomas Nelson are registered trademarks of HarperCollins Christian Publishing, Inc.

Author is represented by The Christopher Ferebee Agency, www.christopherferebee.com.

Thomas Nelson titles may be purchased in bulk for educational, business, fund-raising, or sales promotional use. For information, please e-mail SpecialMarkets@ThomasNelson.com.

Scripture quotations are taken from the Holy Bible, New International Version®, NIV®. Copyright © 1973, 1978, 1984, 2011 by Biblica, Inc.® Used by permission of Zondervan. All rights reserved worldwide. www.Zondervan.com. The "NIV" and "New International Version" are trademarks registered in the United States Patent and Trademark Office by Biblica, Inc.®

Any Internet addresses, phone numbers, or company or product information printed in this book are offered as a resource and are not intended in any way to be or to imply an endorsement by Thomas Nelson, nor does Thomas Nelson vouch for the existence, content, or services of these sites, phone numbers, companies, or products beyond the life of this book.

Library of Congress Cataloging-in-Publication Data

Names: Vaudrey, Scott, author.
Title: Renovate your relationships : a proven guide to setting boundaries and building bridges with those who matter most / Scott Vaudrey, MD, MA.
Description: Nashville, Tennessee : Nelson Books, an imprint of Thomas Nelson, [2019]
Identifiers: LCCN 2018048534 (print) | LCCN 2019014417 (ebook) | ISBN 9781400213351 (TP) | ISBN 9781400213368 (eBook)
Subjects: LCSH: Interpersonal relations--Religious aspects--Christianity.
Classification: LCC BV4597.52 (ebook) | LCC BV4597.52 .V38 2019 (print) | DDC 241/.6762--dc23
LC record available at https://lccn.loc.gov/2018048534

Printed in the United States of America

19 20 21 22 23   LSC   10 9 8 7 6 5 4 3 2 1

To September,
My collaborator for this book—and my life.
You're my favorite person in the world.

Contents

CONTENTS

Part IV: From Start to Finish

A Message for the Reader

M ost of us can think of times when we felt hurt or disappointed by someone who matters to us—a spouse, significant other, family member, coworker, boss, or friend. We ask ourselves:

- "Am I making too big a deal out of this?"
- "Should I just lighten up?"
- "Should I stand up for myself?"
- "How do I draw closer to this person I care about?"
- "How do I create greater safety from this destructive person in my life?"

If one or more of these questions nag at you, good news! By the end of this book, you'll have gained clarity on what you really want in that relationship, and you'll have learned some helpful tools for getting there.

Research has demonstrated with remarkable consistency that the single greatest contribution to our sense of happiness and well-being is the quality of our relationships. This is a book about making relationships better.

We all experience relational challenges from time to time. As you'll see in the pages that follow, I've certainly experienced relational pain firsthand, in both big and small ways. Sometimes I've managed my disappointment well, resulting in relationships that have prevailed and are fulfilling. At other times, sadly, I've over- or underreacted to my disappointment in ways that made matters worse. I've learned a lot from both ends of the spectrum, and this has motivated me to write about what I've discovered along the way.

During my careers as a physician, a pastor, and now an executive coach, I've been given a unique vantage point for spotting patterns that emerge when people find themselves in relational ditches and for identifying helpful strategies to help them get out of those ditches. Speaking about these concepts to groups, organizations, and staff teams has helped me synthesize what I've learned down to its core elements. This book captures these learnings through words, stories, and diagrams, showing how our destructive relational patterns can lead to so much frustration and disappointment, and how we can take steps to create new patterns with people important to us.

The most important part of this process actually happens before we take any step at all. In fact, when we find ourselves frustrated because our boundary setting or bridge building hasn't improved our relational world, in the vast majority of situations the problem isn't our execution but our preparation. A large portion of this book, therefore, focuses on the all-important prep work we must do *before* we engage in bridge-building or boundary-setting conversations, what I also refer to as *accepting* and *protecting*.

This book starts at the beginning. It won't provide you with a quick and temporary fix. Instead, it will guide you in how to take a careful look at all the dynamics at play when a relationship goes off course. Bridge building (accepting) and boundary setting (protecting) will each be examined, and more importantly, you'll learn how to find the right balance between them in every relationship. A practical *Renovate Your Relationships Pathway* chart will guide your progress on the road to renovating your relationships.

Each chapter of this book unpacks the process in increasing depth:

- Part I describes the "problem of life" and explores our potential responses.
- Part II examines several critical mistakes that can get us off track in our relationships. These avoidable errors are the number one cause of boundary- and bridge-building failures.
- Part III establishes how to chart a course of action for improving relationships, while avoiding common pitfalls and managing relational disappointments well. We'll take a deep dive into the actual mechanics of the relational change process—that is, learning to set boundaries—by getting a close-up look at all three stages of boundary setting: before, during, and after. A disproportionate amount of this book is dedicated to setting boundaries and less to building bridges. This is intentional, because when it comes to bridge building, the issue is usually one of awareness. In general, the "how-to" of building bridges is less difficult to discern than the "how-to" of boundary setting. When people realize they need to stand up for themselves and set boundaries, they often lack the "how-to" they need. Part III, therefore, offers a step-by-step coaching in setting boundaries.
- Part IV offers an actual case study that walks you through the entire "renovate your relationships" process in a practical setting.

When I speak at businesses, churches, and nonprofits, people approach me afterward with good questions, and even though my talks are usually about workplace relationships, most of their questions are about family. Most of the examples in this book, therefore, are from family relationships, because those are the relationships that tend to matter most, and peoples' pain is greatest when those relationships break down. But regardless, every principle covered is readily applicable to any relational context—home, work, or elsewhere. I altered the names and identifying details of the individuals in the stories I share to protect their privacy.

My hope is that by the time you turn the last page, you will have a new way of thinking about your relationships and be equipped with tools that will help you when they fail, not just with your current situation, but with every relationship that matters in your life.

Finally, I acknowledge with deep gratitude that this book stands on the shoulders of two must-read books that preceded it: *Boundaries* by Henry Cloud and John Townsend and *Leadership and Self-Deception* by the Arbinger Institute.

S.R.V.
Dundee, Illinois
June 2019

PART I

THE PROBLEM OF LIFE

WHERE WE'RE HEADED:

- What is the "problem of life"?
- The solution
- The two ingredients of healing

We've all been there: a vital relationship is out of alignment. Perhaps the emotional distance between you and the other person feels too vast or the other person's behavior has hurt or disappointed you and some protective distance is needed. This is the relational "problem of life."

Securing safe, fulfilling, and intimate relationships is a central, driving force of human nature. We have a deep, intrinsic longing to be connected to other people, and yet often we find ourselves in situations where relationships fall short of being safe, fulfilling, or intimate.

- Your spouse is drinking too much.
- You feel disconnected from your teenager.
- Your boss is making escalating, excessive demands.
- Your friend has slighted you, again.

The goal of this book is to equip you to move your relationships closer to what you desire them to be. The *Renovate Your Relationships Pathway* chart below gives you an overview of where your relationships are headed, step by step along the journey from disappointment toward building safe, satisfying relationships.

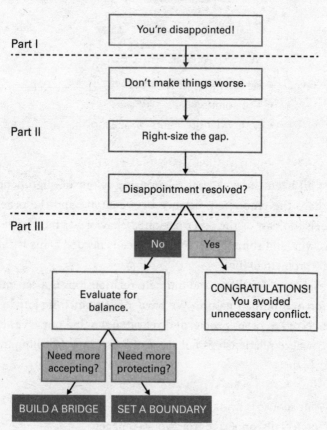

RENOVATE YOUR RELATIONSHIPS PATHWAY

ONE

PROBLEM

Knowing when to build a bridge (accepting) and when to set a boundary (protecting) is the trickiest part of navigating difficult relationships. And that is what this book is all about.

Imagine your twenty-nine-year-old son lives in your basement, plays video games all day, drinks too much, eats your food, works at a part-time minimum-wage job, and doesn't pay rent. His vocational aspirations seem limited to completing the next *Grand Theft Auto* mission, improving his *Call of Duty* infantry skills, and fine-tuning his *Iron Man* costume for the next Comic-Con. When do you set a boundary by insisting he either pay rent or move out? You may fear that setting a boundary too soon—for example, before he has time to find full-time employment—would be unloving, but he's not even trying to look for a better job. You're tormented by the questions: What kind of parent kicks their child out? Who wants that on their conscience?

Imagine your new mother-in-law constantly criticizes you and makes crazy demands on you but not on your spouse or anyone else on her side of the family. Your spouse is used to her behavior and doesn't notice what's going on. But you know you need to set a boundary, and you probably need to ask your spouse to take a more decisive role in protecting you. The question is when. If you set a boundary too quickly, you might alienate your new in-laws, cause added stress to your new marriage, be viewed as a prima donna by your relatives, or ruin the upcoming family barbecue. Who wants that kind of pressure?

Imagine your boss is demanding and insensitive. Although you love the work, you find yourself becoming increasingly resentful and unmotivated. You have a sense that you should say something, but the holidays are coming up and everyone is really busy. Plus, you think you might be up for a promotion soon. Do you risk being stuck in the same role forever or do you say something and risk getting fired? Who wants to enter the holiday season job hunting?

Imagine your friend is going through a hard time. Due to this, your relationship seems to be cooling, and your friendship feels distant. You know she is hurting, but at the same time, you're feeling hurt by the distance. You want to build a bridge of acceptance and move closer, but she is stressed, and you don't want to add to the burden by having a heavy, heartfelt conversation. Plus, you don't want to seem needy or risk being rejected further. Is now the right time to talk?

Imagine your spouse has a problem with anger or substance abuse. His well-established pattern looks like this: blow it, lie about it, get caught, apologize, and promise to do better next time; repeat. You set a boundary some months ago to protect yourself emotionally, and potentially physically, by telling him to move out. Now he seems to be taking responsibility for his life and changing his destructive behaviors. He has joined a twelve-step program, is seeing a therapist, and has not had an angry outburst or abused substances in months. Is now the time to start building a bridge of acceptance by letting him move back home? When is the right time to shift from setting a boundary (staying separated) to building a bridge? Is it too soon to give the relationship another chance? If he fails again, your kids will be heartbroken, and you'll possibly lose their respect for letting it happen, not to mention you'll be heartbroken too. Who wants that burden?

Having close relationships is tricky. German philosopher Arthur

Schopenhauer captured this reality in his parable "the porcupine's dilemma," which is paraphrased as follows:

> A band of porcupines gathered on a cold winter's day. To find relief from the cold—in fact, to avoid freezing to death—the porcupines began to huddle closer together. Their shared warmth brought relief from the chill in the air, but the sharpness of their quills caused each other pain. Soon, the discomfort brought about by close proximity caused the porcupines to move further away from one another. This brought welcomed relief from the painful pokes and stabs. But soon the porcupines began to grow cold.[1]

This dilemma illustrates the tension of intimacy and relationships. If we want to have relationships with others, we must develop and hone our ability to move closer to others, despite the danger of their quills. But there are times we must learn to move farther away, despite the risk of experiencing the cold. This metaphor highlights the necessity of establishing an effective balance between building bridges (accepting) and setting boundaries (protecting).

Relational pain is common to us all. I certainly don't argue this reality. Yet I often behave as if this is only true at a theoretical level. If I'm honest, what I really believe is that relationships are difficult for *other people*. When I experience relational pain, I cry foul; I am shocked and indignant, convinced that there must be some cosmic mistake.

Eugene Peterson, author and theologian, captured this tension beautifully:

> We somehow have ended up a country full of Christians who consider suffering, whether it comes in broken body or in broken heart, a violation of their spiritual rights. If things go badly in body, or job, or family, they whine and complain endlessly.[2]

When I first read this statement from Peterson, I thought, *Whoa, Eugene. A little harsh, don't you think?* But a few months later, when I found myself in a season of relational pain, lo and behold, his description fit me to a tee. I whined and complained endlessly.

This is the relational problem of life. Wherever you find yourself in the tension of Schopenhauer's porcupine dilemma, you're not alone. We all face situations in which we're disappointed by someone. We know something must change in the relationship, but we're not always sure what that something should be. Should we develop thicker skin? Laugh it off? Let it go? Try harder to resolve the issue? Or should we put our foot down and defend ourselves? Create a safer distance? Cool the relationship?

> WE KNOW SOMETHING MUST CHANGE IN THE RELATIONSHIP, BUT WE'RE NOT ALWAYS SURE WHAT THAT SOMETHING SHOULD BE

Which is the right way to handle it? Do we need to build a bridge or set a boundary? Or both? Once we get clarity on the first question—bridge or boundary—we're immediately confronted with an even more difficult question: When?

First When, Then How

Throughout my life—first as an emergency room doctor, then as a pastor,[3] and today as I teach and consult—I know how challenging it can be to answer the question of when. I've felt it myself, and I've sat with thousands of individuals seeking help navigating a challenge in one of their relationships, because they knew the status quo was no longer okay. They would describe their situation, look at me with a pained expression, and then, regardless of the specifics of their circumstances, utter phrases like:

- "I know I should have the hard conversation, but *I just don't know how.*"
- "I know I need to set a boundary, but *I just don't know how.*"
- "I know it's time to set limits, but *I just don't know how.*"

They wisely recognize that something must be "renovated," and they know that in every relationship they have a role to play in making occasional relational repairs to move it toward a healthier place. But not knowing how to make those repairs leaves them paralyzed.

If I press, I often discover an even bigger cause of their paralysis: at some level they actually do know how, just not when to take action. Is it too soon? Should I wait until the next infraction? Should I just lighten up and move on? The *how* is important, but *when* is even more challenging. It's a question they must get right. A problem they must solve.

The Problem of Life

We all experience relational disappointments with people who are important to us. To address these disappointments, we must get a clear, accurate picture of the distance between our desires for the relationship and our current reality.

In healthier relationships, there isn't much distance between our desires and reality. In these relationships, our disappointment is minimal and our relational satisfaction is high. Life is good. The following model captures this concept:

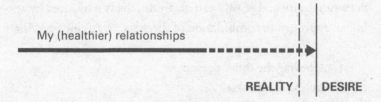

7

But in relationships where there's quite a bit of distance between reality and our desires, our disappointment is far greater. This is the relational problem of life. In the model below, the gap between our desires and reality represents our relational disappointment. Let's give this gap a clever name, "The Gap."

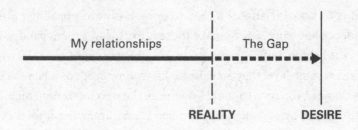

In my life I had seasons with significant gaps with a parent, spouse, or colleague at work. In each of these situations, the distress of the large gap adversely impacted all my other relationships and activities. Unaddressed gaps often fuel anxiety, depression, addiction, and a host of associated bad choices. In important relationships, we spend a significant amount of energy, attention, and ambition trying to minimize this gap. That's why the entirety of part II of this book is devoted to gaining mastery over the three components of our problem of life: reality, desire, and the gap.

Before we engage this important topic, allow me to introduce two more terms: *accepting* and *protecting*. Regardless of the size of our relational gaps, or how much pain they're causing, the space between desire and reality can be productively navigated by applying an appropriate combination of these two strategic ingredients:

1. *Accepting* the other person
2. *Protecting* ourselves

Achieving the ideal balance of accepting others while protecting ourselves from destructive behaviors is the solution to the problem of life and the key to experiencing satisfying relationships. To get there, we must dive deeper into these two necessary ingredients.

TWO

SOLUTION

WHERE WE'RE HEADED:

- Two necessary ingredients: accepting and protecting
- The A/P spectrum: accepting/protecting
- Two types of people: Which type are you?

Which wing of this plane should I use for landing? The left or the right?"

Imagine the pilot of your commercial flight asking this question over the intercom while you're at 30,000 feet. Your answer, along with everyone else's onboard, would be an emphatic, "Both! Use both wings, please! Both are critical!"

This is how I feel after someone shares a relational struggle and then asks, "Should I build a bridge (accept) or set a boundary (protect)?" Both are critical.

Two Necessary Ingredients

Ideally, in every relational scenario, we want to both accept (not make a bigger deal than necessary) and protect (guard the dignity and safety of all parties). The trick is finding the perfect balance between the two. What ratio of accepting and protecting will bring the desired outcome?

We'll define and explore both ingredients in greater detail in chapters 3 and 4. For now, let's generalize these terms as follows:

- *Accepting:* building a bridge toward another person
- *Protecting:* setting a boundary

A Car Analogy

Every car with an automatic transmission has two vitally important pedals: the gas pedal and the brake. To drive successfully, you need to regularly and consistently use both pedals in right measure.

Driving on an interstate highway when traffic is light, you'll probably use the gas pedal more often than the brake pedal (see Figure A below). Driving into a congested intersection to turn left, you'll probably use the brake pedal more often than the gas pedal (Figure B).

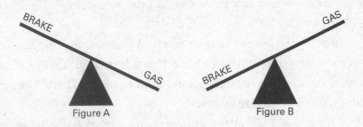

Figure A   Figure B

Driving mandates the use of both pedals. And we must consistently apply the ideal balance in different situations to reach our destination successfully, and without harm to ourselves or others. The same is true in our relational journeys. We must consistently apply the ideal balance of the two ingredients when managing our gaps. But how much of each strategy is ideal? What's the right balance in each situation?

If a relational disappointment is mild, uncommon, or less

costly—for example, if a trusted coworker is a little late in completing his part of the project, or if a child does a slightly less than stellar job at one of her chores—the ideal balance might require more accepting (bridge building), with maybe a small dose of protecting (boundary setting). If we react too strongly to mild relational gaps, we're guilty of *over-protecting*, and we risk harming those relationships. Those who tend to over-protect should remind themselves, "I don't need to make a big deal about this."

If a relational disappointment is significant, ongoing, or places someone in danger, as in domestic violence, drunk driving, or any criminal activity, the ideal balance will likely be a lot of protecting and almost no accepting. When we fail to stand up against these types of infractions, we're guilty of *over-accepting*. Those prone to letting things slide must remind themselves, "Yes, I do need to make a big deal about this right now!"

THE ACCEPTING/PROTECTING (A/P) SPECTRUM

In most situations, though, our relational gaps fall somewhere in between these two extremes. How do we know if we've found the ideal balance of accepting and protecting when the situation is less clear? The *Accepting/Protecting (A/P) Spectrum* diagram below helps bring clarity to what the ideal balance looks like in any given situation:

ACCEPTING/PROTECTING (A/P) SPECTRUM

| ACCEPT | Destructively Over-Accepting Under-Protecting | Over-Accepting Under-Protecting | IDEAL BALANCE | Over-Protecting Under-Accepting | Destructively Over-Protecting Under-Accepting | PROTECT |

When you're dealing with the disappointment of a relational gap perfectly, your ideal balance of accepting and protecting would land in the center of the diagram. Being in the center zone of the A/P spectrum doesn't mean applying *equal* amounts of accepting and protecting—50 percent accepting plus 50 percent protecting—rather, it means applying the *ideal* amounts. If your situation is extreme, such as when someone will be physically harmed if you don't take a stand, and you apply a balance of 99 percent protecting and 1 percent accepting, you've chosen an ideal balance. Similarly, if your gap is mild, such as when someone has apologized after causing you mild disappointment, which is out of character for that person, and you apply a balance of 99 percent accepting and 1 percent protecting, you've chosen an ideal balance.

In both cases, you've reached the balance most likely to lead to healthier relationships. A center-zone position always helps you minimize your relational gap.

The Center Zone: Ideal Balance of Accepting and Protecting

How can you tell if you're in that ideal center zone? When you're responding with the ideal measure of accepting and protecting for a given situation, regardless of whether that means primarily building a bridge or primarily setting a boundary, your response toward the other person is consistently marked by the following characteristics:

- Clear
- Respectful
- Reasonable
- Kind
- Courageous
- Fosters a healthier relationship

When all parties are treated with dignity and your response can be described using these words, you're in that sweet center zone.

Applying an ideal balance of accepting and protecting is the only way to simultaneously manage your disappointments and strengthen your relationships. The center zone builds trust and safety.

Sometimes it's hard to be sure that your response is in the center zone. Often, it's easier to notice when you're not in the center and you feel the need to adjust. Whenever you step away from an ideal balance of accepting and protecting, you widen the gap of your relational disappointment and eventually make things worse. It's like driving a car and applying more brake or more gas than needed for a given traffic situation—you crash. When you've moved away from center and into the gray or black zones of the A/P spectrum, you cause harm to yourself and your relationships.

To better understand this idea, see the expanded A/P spectrum below, which includes details of each zone:

ACCEPTING/PROTECTING (A/P) SPECTRUM

ACCEPT				PROTECT
Destructively Over-Accepting Under-Protecting	Over-Accepting Under-Protecting	**IDEAL BALANCE**	Over-Protecting Under-Accepting	Destructively Over-Protecting Under-Accepting
PLEASERS →			← DEFENDERS	
Exploited Checked out Codependent Resentful Weak	Complacent People pleasing Capitulating Martyr Passive	Clear Reasonable Kind Courageous Satisfied	Controlling Intolerant Smug Critical Rigid	Aggressive Punitive Contentious Abandoning Manipulating
SELF-DESTRUCTIVE	SELF-DEPRIVING	SELF-RESPECTING	SELF-RIGHTEOUS	SELF-CENTERED

Over-Protecting: When Helping Becomes Controlling

If you use more protecting than called for, then you've moved toward the right side of the A/P spectrum, into the area labeled "Over-Protecting." By definition, this means you're also under-accepting the other person. And if you choose extreme amounts of protecting, you've stepped into the far-right zone labeled "Destructively Over-Protecting."

Over-protecting behavior can be subtle at first. You may be able to convince yourself and others that you're just trying to help the other person by offering input and advice. But eventually you receive feedback from others that you're impatient, impossible to please, or intolerant. Left unchecked, your over-protecting behavior will manifest itself as rigid and controlling.

Clues that we're venturing into the right side of the spectrum (over-protecting) often come from how other people respond to us. Initially, our over-protecting can lead others to feel sad and insecure in the relationship. Over time, these emotions often develop into frustration and underlying resentment toward us for our under-accepting behaviors and attitudes. Eventually, this resentment will leak out; people may begin to fight back or show passive-aggressive resistance toward our attempts to control. Their resistance typically heightens our over-protecting behaviors, and we enter into a downward spiral of ever-increasing relational pain. One of the most dangerous characteristics of over-protecting is an associated self-righteousness that leaves us blind to our profound contribution to this destructive cycle. But no matter the pain, we persist in our certainty that the problem is them, not us.

At its worst, over-protecting utilizes a dangerous brand of control and critique that is abusive toward the other person. When we are being over-protecting to the point of verbal, emotional, spiritual, sexual, or physical abuse, our self-righteousness often remains intact despite the harm we're causing. We become so self-absorbed that we justify our abusive behavior as a reasonable way to get our needs met, even at the expense of the other person's well-being.

Over-Accepting: When "Nice" Isn't So Nice

If you are more accepting than is helpful to the situation, then you've moved toward the left side of the A/P spectrum, into the zone labeled "Over-Accepting." This likely means you're under-protecting yourself or over-accepting the other person. And if you really tip the scales on accepting, such as submitting yourself to harm from the behavior of another person, you've crossed over into the far-left zone labeled "Destructively Over-Accepting."

Like over-protecting, over-accepting behavior can be subtle at first. You may convince yourself that you're just "being nice," you're giving the other person the benefit of the doubt, or you're just being extra patient, waiting for the right time to act—except the right time never comes. Soon your behavior slips into the "self-depriving" category on the A/P spectrum.

Self-depriving differs from mere self-sacrifice. When we make appropriate sacrifices for those we love, we often feel content and satisfied. Self-depriving behavior, on the other hand, leaves us damaged. We feel used, rather than satisfied. Mutually sacrificial relationships are life-giving, but when our conduct slips into self-depriving, we feel a little emptier with each sacrifice. If we continue down the self-depriving path, eventually we become depleted and resentful.

When we over-accept, we end up submitting to an increasingly unhealthy level of self-sacrifice. Giving someone the benefit of the doubt and being patient are all good things; over-accepting someone's bad behavior is not. What may have started as a self-respecting kindness toward someone who has hurt us will shift, if left unchecked, toward people pleasing. This will keep us from doing what we know is best and right.

WHEN WE OVER-ACCEPT, WE END UP SUBMITTING TO AN INCREASINGLY UNHEALTHY LEVEL OF SELF-SACRIFICE.

Clues that we've drifted toward the left side of the spectrum (over-accepting) include feedback from friends or family that might sound like this:

- "Stand up for yourself!"
- "Don't put up with that!"

- "She's walking all over you!"
- "He's taking advantage of you!"

If these comments sound familiar, it may be a sign you're over-accepting in a key relationship. Over-acceptors tend to tell themselves that they're just being "too nice." But being nice is always a good, productive thing; being "too nice" is not. Over-accepting isn't a productive way of managing relationships. If you sense you fall into the category of over-accepting, try to find an accurate phrase to describe what's really going on.

Phrases might be: "I'm too afraid to say or do the right thing," or "I'm afraid if I stand up for myself, I'll be rejected." Fear is often at the center of why we over-accept. Sometimes it's reasonable to feel a little fear when we know we need to shift to a more protecting posture. We fear losing the relationship, or we fear the reaction of the other person if we do the right thing. Indeed, this type of loss is a legitimate possibility when we enter this space.

Life isn't necessarily easier when we live with a more ideal balance of accepting and protecting, but life is better. When we're afraid to resist or speak up, then by definition, our compliance isn't a choice. As Henry Cloud puts it, "When we are afraid to say no, our yes is compromised."[1]

This leads us to another clue that over-accepting may be a problem: You feel self-pity or resentment toward the other person. You wonder why the other person doesn't notice or appreciate your sacrifice. Or you start responding passive-aggressively toward that person.

Over-accepting often shows itself through a destructive codependence on the other person that de-emphasizes our own needs, dignity, and even safety. Over time, over-acceptors are at risk of allowing themselves to be taken advantage of. At best, they're not appreciated, which is self-depriving. At worst, they experience outright abuse, which is self-destructive (the far-left side of the A/P spectrum).

Even though my tendency is toward over-protection, I have the capacity to resort to both over-protecting and over-accepting. I recall with regret the times when I gave in to an overly aggressive attending physician or supervisor and failed to adequately defend myself or others. My guess is that you can think of such times in your life as well.

WHERE ARE YOU ON THE A/P SPECTRUM?

Think of a current relationship you sense is out of balance. Where do you see yourself on the A/P spectrum? Whether your response swings left or right, you can move toward that ideal center balance by adding more of the underrepresented ingredient to the mix. While the characteristics listed in the A/P spectrum aren't 100 percent all-inclusive, they can help you gauge your balance of accepting and protecting.

Think through your most difficult relationship and answer the following questions:

- How would moving toward the ideal center balance change your conversations and arguments?
- How would a commitment to living in the ideal balance of accepting and protecting change those times when you get stuck?
- How would living in an ideal balance build hope and safety into your relationship?
- How much better would it be if you were consistently kind and courageous, even when it means saying or doing hard things?

Of course, you must not be naive. Sometimes when you make a change in the status quo, the relationship gets worse before it gets better. In some situations, the destructive behavior of the other person requires greater distance between the two of you. But a healthy distance is ultimately better for you both.

Knowing Yourself

Most people find that when it comes to the two ingredients of accepting and protecting, one ingredient comes more naturally than the other. Often, one ingredient is their go-to tool when relationships get uncomfortable. However, we can all think of exceptions to the rule: in some relational contexts we tend to over-accept, while in others we're more likely to over-protect.

Understanding the context is key. For example, it's common for people to over-accept with their supervisors at work but to over-protect with their spouses at home. Often, the power differential comes into play. In relationships where a person holds a degree of power over us, we're more likely to over-accept their bad behavior; whereas in relationships where we hold more power, or where the playing field is more even, we might over-protect.

At times within the same relationship, we may swing back and forth. I've had situations in my marriage where I was way over-accepting and did not stand up for myself; and in that same season, I was way over-protecting, resorting to being controlling and hurtful.

Most of us tend to gravitate toward one strategy over the other based on our upbringing, temperament, and life experience. We're either primarily accepting or primarily protecting. As a result, we often apply our preferred ingredient early and often, sometimes too early and too often to be helpful. Which is it for you?

Part of how I learned to cope with disappointments in my life was to try to control the world. When I get off balance, it's almost always toward the right side of the spectrum. I'm an over-protector by nature. Obviously, this has proven to be a futile and unhealthy pattern; it doesn't build better relationships.

This tendency has reared its ugly head in many areas of my life, especially with my wife and kids, as you'll see throughout this book.

But my work life also has been impacted by my tendency to over-protect. I remember a time when I needed to give some negative feedback to one of my direct reports in the emergency department. When this physician responded defensively and aggressively toward me, I reacted with impatience and promptly increased my level of control over his work in the coming weeks by reviewing and auditing his patient care more aggressively. Paradoxically, as I increased my control, I also distanced myself relationally and avoided working directly with him whenever possible. My partners could sense the tension between us. While some protection from this physician's antipathy toward me was appropriate, I now realize that my over-protecting response resulted in an avoidable relational rift that rippled through the entire department.

Sometimes our go-to strategy is just what the situation needs, and a relational gap becomes smaller. But, inevitably, there are times when our go-to strategy is exactly *not* what is needed, and our natural reflexive response makes matters worse.

Having a natural tendency for one ingredient over the other is normal, and one ingredient isn't better than the other—they're value neutral. They both serve vitally important roles in our relationships. But it's important to identify which type of person you are—a natural acceptor or a natural protector—because it's human nature to over-use the ingredient that comes easiest to us.

Routinely relying on only your preferred ingredient is a costly mistake, although common and avoidable. Knowing your natural tendency is essential to managing your relational gaps and obtaining your desired results. If you fail to pay attention to your go-to strategy, you'll be less likely to notice when you overuse it, even when it leaves you far to the left or right of an ideal balance in the relationship.

If you're in the habit of doing what comes easiest or most naturally when relationships leave you disappointed, you're normal; it's how most of us have always operated. But if the only tool in your toolbox is a hammer, every problem becomes a nail. Why not learn to use both strategies fluently? By doubling the number of tools in your toolbox, you can choose the most *effective* tool to bring your relationships toward that sweet center zone in every situation.

Acceptors: Over-Accepting Plus Under-Protecting

For some people, what comes naturally in relationships is to be accepting. Their natural wiring, family upbringing, and past experiences leave them prone to building bridges, regardless of anyone else's behavior. If this describes you, at your best, you're patient, resilient, flexible, and content. You're not easily offended. You don't jump to conclusions or make a big deal when things don't go your way. You're an easy person to be with, and people might call you relaxed and easygoing. In general, you're more of an acceptor.

As an acceptor, sometimes you can be too accommodating. You naturally tend toward over-accepting others and under-protecting yourself. Perhaps you've been labeled as a bit of a pushover or even weak. For a number of reasons, you're too slow to protect yourself and too quick to tolerate the bad behaviors of others, even when that behavior is destructive. Accepting other people comes naturally to you, and it's much more difficult to protect yourself or others.

The relational strategy of over-accepting/under-protecting is typically learned in childhood to cope with or survive our families of origin, and it's an effective short-term strategy for avoiding conflict. But over-accepting is a poor long-term strategy for finding relational satisfaction and contentment.

Acceptors often find it daunting to set boundaries, preferring rather to build bridges. Sadly, some acceptors don't recognize when their own dignity, value, or safety is threatened by someone else's behavior. They're slow to see the point where building a bridge is no longer helpful and actually increases their relational pain.

Some acceptors find themselves stuck in a pattern of being destructively over-accepting and codependent. When they over-accept and under-protect, they invite harm to themselves and others, including the person whose behavior is destructive. By allowing such behavior to continue unabated, acceptors protect the offenders from the natural consequences of their behavior, thus putting themselves, others, and even the offenders at greater risk in the long term.

Most acceptors have an intuition that their over-accepting and under-protecting are real problems. They catch clues both *internally* (they recognize that they don't advocate for themselves, they feel like a martyr, or they become resentful) and *externally* (they hear feedback that they're overindulgent and should defend themselves more). If you're catching clues like this, pay attention. Being an acceptor puts you in a vulnerable position and will never bring you the safe, meaningful relationships you desire.

I recognize that for many, shifting to a more protecting posture comes with real risk. As we discussed earlier, the relationship may get harder before it gets better. Or worse, things may not get better, in which case a persistent self-protective distance is in order. This prospect can be terrifying. We don't want to be alone or face the anger of the other person. But while these risks are real, I have confidence that in the long term, even these rare extreme outcomes would be better for you relationally than the status quo.

Do you wonder if you're an acceptor with a blind spot? See the "Assess: Are You an Acceptor?" box for a couple of diagnostic strategies to help see yourself more clearly.

ASSESS: ARE YOU AN ACCEPTOR?

Ask Yourself

Take some time and review the internal emotions and convictions you feel when someone isn't behaving well around you. Are there any themes? Many acceptors can recall a sense of shame over their lack of courage, that "stronger people would have stood up for themselves." Others recall feeling fear of rejection if they stand up for themselves. Do you have any insight into whether or not you tend to over-accept? Can your tendency to "give others the benefit of the doubt" be more accurately described as your tendency to avoid addressing the real issue?

Ask Others

People who know you well can often spot patterns in your life quicker than you can spot them yourself. It has been my experience that if you make it safe and easy for trusted friends and family to give you feedback, they will do so. Ask for their input, using specific, clear questions, such as the following:

- Am I over-accepting of other people at times?
- Do you think I am slow to defend or advocate for myself?
- Have there been times when you wished I had behaved more courageously?
- Do I avoid conflict?
- Do you think I put up with too much mistreatment from others?

Protectors: Over-Protecting Plus Under-Accepting

Others, based on natural wiring, upbringing, and life experience, tend to be too quick to protect themselves and too slow to accept the choices or behaviors of others. They are more comfortable overusing the protecting ingredient and underusing the accepting ingredient. In general, they're *protectors*.

Protectors learned at an early age that setting boundaries for safety, or the illusion of safety, brings comfort, and that strength or control is the shortest pathway to safety. If this describes you, at your best, people describe you as strong and forthright. At your worst, they might label you as intolerant, hypersensitive, controlling, or even a bully.

Protectors have a core fear of being exploited. They quickly and frequently stand up for themselves, even if doing so widens the relational gap. They tend to respond with an external posture that suggests anger, intimidation, and power, even though inside they're often more frightened than angry. Being a protector is a pretty effective strategy for avoiding exploitation, but as a strategy for finding sustained relational satisfaction, it can be a real problem.

For protectors, the idea of building a bridge can be daunting. It triggers their core fears of being hurt or taken advantage of. When they respond by protecting themselves, even when their relational disappointments don't present a legitimate threat to their dignity, value, or safety, they move from "setting a healthy boundary" to over-protecting and under-accepting, which sabotages their relationships.

I am a protector. So I can tell you from experience that, sadly, we protectors are less likely to be self-aware of how problematic our behavior can be. Because of the odd combination of confidence and fear that most protectors possess, we're much more likely to miss the obvious and not acknowledge our contributions to our relational gaps. We're more likely to have a blind spot when it comes to seeing that we tend to over-protect and under-accept when disappointed.

Do you wonder if you're a protector with a blind spot? See the "Assess: Are You a Protector?" box for a couple of diagnostic strategies to help see yourself more clearly.

ASSESS: ARE YOU A PROTECTOR?

Ask Yourself

Be honest with yourself about the feedback you've received through the years after hard conversations. Are there any themes? For me, there was one simple phrase that I heard over and over, no matter the circumstance, mostly from my wife, but from friends and colleagues as well: "Do you really have to make such a big deal about this?" Hearing this question repeatedly was the clue I needed to help me see my blind spot and admit that I over-protect and under-accept when dealing with my relational gaps.

Take plenty of time and really process the issues. Ask yourself the following questions:

- Do I tend to be defensive or reactive?
- Am I quick to protest or defend myself?
- Do I sometimes overreact when I feel slighted?
- Do people sometimes comment that I have a thin skin?
- How do I respond when others react to slights from me the way I responded to theirs?

Ask Others

This is tricky because the more you over-protect and under-accept, the less safe others feel in giving you honest feedback, even when you ask for it. Ask anyway. Make them feel safe by assuring them that you suspect you might have a blind spot in this area and you need their perspective. Ask them questions, such as the following:

- Am I over-protective?
- Am I controlling?
- Am I prone to get mad easily?
- Am I a little too quick to defend myself?
- Do you find me to be intolerant at times?
- Am I overly sensitive to criticisms or slights?
- Do I seem a little paranoid at times?

If the person you're seeking honest feedback from hesitates before answering, you have your answer. It's yes. You're probably a little over-protective, controlling, intolerant, overly sensitive, and paranoid. In short, you—like me—are a protector. Welcome to the club.

A Story from the Home Front

My lovely wife, September, places herself in the acceptor category, and I concur. She's generally relaxed, accepting, and able to give people the benefit of the doubt. She has an amazing ability not to make a big deal about things, and as such, she's an amazing bridge builder toward others in her world. Accepting always has come easy for her, and it's a beautiful quality in the right balance. But sometimes September tends to over-accept and under-protect when she's disappointed with someone.

Like most of us, September learned to excel using this one ingredient (accepting) over the other (protecting) during her growing-up years. As the only sibling of a special-needs younger brother, she learned to be a peacemaker in an environment where her brother directed his frustrations and aggression toward her. Today, September is still more likely to not make waves than to stand up for herself. Choosing her legitimate needs over the needs of another person makes her uncomfortable and requires intentionality on her part.

As I mentioned, I'm more of a protector. It's easier for me to set boundaries than to build bridges. Like my wife, I learned to excel using this one ingredient in my growing-up years, where my dad was a protector like me, and my mom was more of an acceptor. From an early age, I developed skills at shielding myself with boundaries as a way to feel safe and in control. I'm still an intense person who tends to react to problems quickly. This is a strength when I'm using it in helpful ways. But sometimes I react too quickly and can be impatient, critical, and a bit paranoid about perceived slights or criticisms. I must constantly ask myself, Am I spotting relational danger when none is present?

September and I have not overcome our natural go-to tendencies toward being acceptors or protectors. Rather, we try to understand these parts of ourselves and catch ourselves when we're slipping to the left or right of center in any given situation. September tries to catch herself from dipping into the pattern of pleaser by asking herself the simple question, Does this situation call for me to stand up for myself? And I try to temper my protector leanings by asking myself, Do I need to make a big deal about this?

What's Your Go-To Strategy?

Which comes easier for you: accepting or protecting? No matter which camp you fall into, take heart. Acceptors can learn to move from the left side of the A/P spectrum into that sweet center zone, and protectors can learn to move from the right. You can learn to have a more balanced response, even in the most difficult relational disappointments. The rest of this book is dedicated to equipping you to do so.

Let's begin by gaining a deeper understanding of accepting, the strategy of bridge building.

THREE

ACCEPTING: WHEN BRIDGE BUILDING IS THE IDEAL STRATEGY

WHERE WE'RE HEADED:

- The value of accepting
- The tasks of accepting:
  - Before your response
  - During your response
  - After your response

M ight you be overreacting just a bit?!"

I get this question a lot. Thankfully less today than when I was younger. This is code from my friends and loved ones to remind me of my tendency to over-protect in situations that actually call for greater amounts of accepting.

All our human relationships have imperfect parts. While there will be times when someone important to you is clearly in the wrong—physically threatening you, treating you in demeaning ways, or making immoral choices—most of the time the issue behind your disappointment isn't a flagrant foul or a clear-cut moral violation but a clash of value-neutral desires, preferences that are neither right nor wrong but simply mismatched from the desires or preferences of the other person. In these cases, insisting that you're right and the other person is wrong will only make matters worse.

John M. Gottman is one of the most celebrated and published academics in the field of intimate relationships. His books and articles focus on married couples, but his findings correlate well to all relationships. In his research on conflict between married couples, he discovered that a whopping 69 percent of the time, their disagreements are about value-neutral preferences. The take-home message for us is that the majority of our relational disappointments aren't about issues with a clear right-or-wrong position. Yet the belief that

VALUE-NEUTRAL ISSUES	
IN MARRIAGE OR ROMANTIC PARTNERSHIPS	**IN WORK, FRIENDSHIPS, OR OTHER RELATIONSHIPS**
How and when to discipline a child	How to reward subordinates
Early to bed or early to rise	How to address a relative's smoking
How much money to put into savings	Emphasizing quality or quantity
How often to have sex	What type of music to play
Where to go for a vacation	Structured or unstructured staff meetings
Fast food or sit-down restaurant	How often a grown child should call home or a parent should check in
How tidy to keep the house	Democrat or Republican
Who does which chores	How much dog barking is too much
How much time to spend with friends or family	How much to spend on employee recognition
What to watch on TV or how much TV to watch	Expectations during busy seasons at work
When to open Christmas presents	Which jokes are funny
Mexican food or Chinese food	Who will host Thanksgiving dinner

one of us is right and the other is wrong often animates our feuds and keeps our gaps perpetually wide.

Gottman's findings suggest that disagreements rooted in value-neutral positions should not have a goal of determining a clear winner and loser. On the previous page, you'll see examples of value-neutral issues that frequently crop up in relationships.

More often than not, when disagreements over these types of issues are addressed with a strategy of primarily accepting and not making a big deal, they will lead to better relationships. When you encounter a disappointment and plan a response that is mostly accepting, there is work to do before, during, and after you respond in an accepting manner.

BEFORE YOUR RESPONSE

1. Remember Your Own Capacity to Disappoint Others

When I face a difficult relational gap, it's easy for me to focus on the other person's bad behavior and conveniently forget about my own patterns of conduct that are often equally bad. Knowing this about myself, whenever I'm disappointed in someone I try to remember all the ways I can be a challenge to others. This isn't *excusing* the other person's misconduct, it's simply a discipline to help me *categorize* their behavior correctly. So when I'm disappointed with a direct report at work, and I'm preparing to respond with my typical over-protecting posture, I first remind myself that my own choices and temperament frequently disappoint my teammates.

For example, one dearly loved, gifted pastor, Chris, who reports to me, tends to be slow to embrace change. I, on the other hand, love change. There are times in our work relationship when I get frustrated with this aspect of Chris's personality, because change is my favorite part of work. So, before I give voice to my frustration, I ask myself, How difficult is it for Chris to have me as a boss?

I'm immediately reminded of the reality that my team must make adjustments frequently to accommodate my love for change. I can expect a collective, loving eye roll from the whole group whenever I get a new idea. While it (hopefully) results in better programs, it always means more work. I'm sure this frustrates them on a regular basis. My desire to tweak and improve is usually a good thing, but sometimes it's me overusing a strength that frustrates my team.

After examining my own disappointing behavior in the area of change, it's easier to remind myself that Chris's tendency to resist change is his overusing his strength—counting the cost, being sensitive to how the change will affect others, and making sure the change is worth it. When I sense a need to respond to Chris's caution with increased levels of protecting, by insisting on the needed change, I first remind myself that it's not always easy to have me as a boss. This usually helps me keep from over-protecting and controlling the situation. Our differing tendencies actually make us great partners. We balance each other.

By doing your best to see yourself from the other person's point of view, you'll be less likely to over-protect (or accept). We all have a capacity to disappoint others, so remembering this helps us to treat others with kindness, rather than control.

2. Give the Other Person the Benefit of the Doubt

Many of us protectors tend to "catastrophize" situations when we feel disappointed. The discipline of giving the other person the benefit of the doubt helps temper our tendency to see only the worst in them.

If I send an email to someone and he is slow to respond, it tweaks a tiny, broken part of me that interprets his slow response as, "He's mad at me" or "He's being passive-aggressive," when, in fact, most of the time the other person is simply busy. Those of us in this catastrophizing camp have an overactive internal alert system that quickly—and often inaccurately—interprets relational exchanges as hurtful or disrespectful when they're neither. Our internal alert isn't aligned with reality.

When in doubt, your first response to new disappointment should be primarily accepting of the other person, so long as you're not jeopardizing anyone's dignity, value, or safety by choosing not to make a big deal, move toward peace, and build bridges. We cannot hope to have rewarding relationships that prevail without developing the habit of accepting and building bridges whenever possible.

When we wrong someone and that person offers a primarily accepting response to us, we savor that feeling of grace received. We often feel closer to that person and are grateful for their bridge-building efforts. The same is true in reverse: when we apply more accepting than protecting to our gaps, people generally value the kindness we extend.

We should accept the other person and their imperfections, as we hope that person accepts us and our imperfections.

3. Behave Like There Is Hope for Change

In his clever book *I Hear You*, mediation expert and consultant Donny Ebenstein offers an analogy that helps illustrate the power of behaving as if there is hope for change: the crossword puzzle.

Imagine you're in the middle of completing a difficult crossword puzzle and you're stuck and frustrated. How would you respond if you were to learn that in 30–40 percent of all crossword puzzles, there is no solution? You'd tell yourself, "This must be one of those unsolvable crossword puzzles," and quit. Or at least I would.

In reality, however, we know that all crossword puzzles have solutions. This is why we keep trying when they get hard. Because the problem has an answer, we work hard to get unstuck and back on track. This is the posture we should take in our relationships: behave as if there is a solution. It's incredibly rare to have a relational disappointment that does not have an effective, redemptive solution that will narrow the gap and bring greater satisfaction. Therefore, let's be slow to throw in the towel when we feel stuck.

During Your Response

The second stage of accepting—your actual response to the other person—has only two tasks:

1. Acknowledge your disappointment
2. Don't make a big deal about it

These tasks seem straightforward, but they aren't as simple as they may appear. Both of these tasks present subtle challenges. For one thing, both conflicting parties must decide which direction they want to go on the given issue; you reach a compromise or agree that one person gets their way this time. Regardless of the decision, the process outlined in the "Before" stage is what helps you manage the gap of disappointment well.

The two vital tasks in this "During" stage present subtle challenges, for both acceptors and protectors. Acceptors, who don't like to make a big deal about being disappointed to begin with, might be tempted to skip the first task: acknowledging their disappointment to the other person. After all, self-advocacy means risking a strong reaction or even rejection from the other person. Why bother taking that risk if you aren't planning on doing anything about it? Isn't that just making a bigger deal than is necessary?

Protectors, too, face temptations in this stage. Giving voice to their disappointment isn't hard for them, but the second task—don't make a big deal—can be tough. Protectors fear that failing to deliver a strong response to their disappointment might positively reinforce bad behavior in the other person and leave themselves at risk for future exploitation.

At first glance, the protests from both sides hold merit. But let's look at these tasks more carefully to understand why each one is so vital, both for acceptors and protectors.

1. Acknowledge Your Disappointment

When you take the time to give voice to your disappointment, you receive two important benefits: you get to recalibrate your expectations or desires with the other person, and you get to practice giving voice to your desires and standing up for yourself while the stakes are low.

Naming Your Disappointment Recalibrates Your Expectations

Giving voice to your disappointment helps you check in with the other person and get an answer to the question, "Is my interpretation of what's going on consistent with your interpretation?" When you acknowledge your disappointment, the person who disappointed you knows that, at some level, there's a gap between your desires and the current reality. If you remain silent, the other person has no way of knowing you felt any disappointment at all. By naming your disappointment, you can test your interpretation of the situation before choosing how to respond, which will help you avoid responding in a way that damages the relationship or makes matters worse.

Recalibrating expectations by acknowledging disappointments is an important discipline for acceptors, who may otherwise remain silent until an infraction is repeated a number of times—at which point the other person can rightly respond, "I had no idea this bothered you. Why didn't you tell me sooner?" If we fail to give voice to our disappointment,

> GIVING VOICE TO YOUR DISAPPOINTMENT HELPS YOU CHECK IN WITH THE OTHER PERSON AND GET AN ANSWER TO THE QUESTION, "IS MY INTERPRETATION OF WHAT'S GOING ON CONSISTENT WITH YOUR INTERPRETATION?"

however slight, the situation is at risk for repeating itself and becoming a pattern that can erode the relationship for the long haul.

When acknowledging our disappointment, we should do so without edge, drama, or inflammatory words. With genuine curiosity, we should seek to learn rather than to win. And we should wait for the other person's response, since their reaction will provide important data that can guide us as we discern how much accepting and protecting is needed for the situation.

What does it sound like to acknowledge your disappointment in a way that invites helpful feedback from the other person? Below are some helpful examples:

HOW ACKNOWLEDGING DISAPPOINTMENT CAN RIGHT-SIZE REALITY

YOU	OTHER PERSON	NEW REALITY
I'm disappointed that I haven't received an answer to the email I sent you yesterday.	I didn't receive an email from you yesterday. My most recent email from you was last Tuesday.	Dang. I forgot to hit Send.
I'm disappointed you didn't call sooner to tell me you were going to be late.	I'm so sorry. Our route took us out of cell phone range. I called as soon as I got a signal.	She wasn't being inconsiderate; she just couldn't get phone reception.
I'm bummed that you finalized the plans without first talking to me.	I called you three times, but you didn't answer, so I left messages. I couldn't wait any longer to make a decision.	Dang. I didn't get her calls because my ringer was turned off.
I'm sad that you left for the concert without me.	Sorry, but I decided to go to the show with Andy.	He doesn't want me to accompany him as much as I'd hoped.
I'm surprised you gave the project to Fred when you'd told me I would be the lead on it.	Yes, but Fred practically begged me for the project, and I figured you wouldn't mind.	My boss may not be able to stand up to pressure from Fred.

In the first three examples, your disappointment might *decrease* considerably once you understand the circumstances more accurately. With a new right-sized reality you'd likely offer a fully accepting response that would narrow or eliminate that gap in the relationship.

In the last two examples, your disappointment would be validated and might even *increase* because you've gained a more accurate understanding of how this person treated you. You might still choose a primarily accepting response to the current situation, but if a pattern emerges, you'll likely apply more protecting than accepting in future interactions. In both cases, acknowledging your disappointment provided you with valuable data.

For those of us who are protectors, recalibrating our initial interpretations of a situation by naming our disappointments is also useful, but for different reasons. Gathering data from the other person helps us avoid overreacting to slight infractions. By discovering that we have misinterpreted a situation *before* we overreact, we avoid repeating our familiar pattern of being overly sensitive, jumping to conclusions, and causing harm to a relationship.

But even if we protectors discover that the other person's actions were just as hurtful as we feared, giving voice to our disappointment helps us feel heard and understood. Instead of responding with knee-jerk aggression, we can choose to respond with dignity, courage, and kindness. If, after our initial efforts at accepting, we learn that a higher percentage of protecting is actually in order, then we can proceed toward boundary setting, confident that this situation isn't one of those times when we "made too big of a deal."

A Story from the Home Front: Late Again

Here's a more personal example of how recalibrating expectations plays out. My wife, September, is an intelligent, warm, joyful, capable woman who did the lion's share of running the house and raising our five kids, while I worked my way through medical school, residency, and my job as an attending physician in the emergency department.

She's also an avid gardener, wood carver, quilter, and leatherworker; she cooks and hosts for large gatherings in our home without effort; and she's a gifted author, teacher, and editor. In short, September is one of the most competent and amazing people I know.

Except in one area.

For the first good chunk of our marriage, one of the more vexing themes to our disagreements was punctuality. Let's just say that September has a relaxed relationship with time. I, on the other hand, believe that "on time" means five minutes early. Here's how this theme played out in the early years of our marriage.

We would agree to meet somewhere for lunch. I would get myself ready, leave with plenty of minutes to spare, and arrive at the *correct* time, that is, five minutes early. September would often arrive ten or fifteen minutes late. The verbal volley that would then ensue often went like this:

Me: Where were you? I've been waiting here for half an hour! (Slight exaggeration, granted.)

September: Long lines at Costco. I got here as soon as I could.

Me: You knew I was waiting. You're so insensitive!

September: I had lots of errands. You're so intolerant!

Me: Why can't you plan better?!

September: Why can't you lighten up?!

And so another round of the "Vaudrey punctuality versus flexibility" spiral would begin. Over the years, September let me know that, while she knew it wasn't okay to be late as often as she was (it was insensitive and caused a gap between us), my reaction to her tardiness was controlling, smug, and intolerant, and created an *even greater* gap.

Once I recognized that my angry reaction to September's lateness was over-protecting, I knew I needed to shift toward the center on the A/P spectrum. If I were to plot my overreactions, I'd have landed solidly in the over-protecting or destructively over-protecting zone.

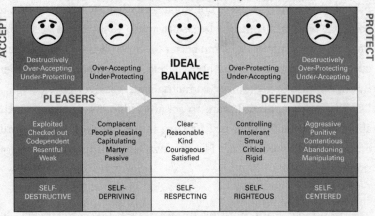

ACCEPTING/PROTECTING (A/P) SPECTRUM

ACCEPT					PROTECT
Destructively Over-Accepting Under-Protecting	Over-Accepting Under-Protecting	**IDEAL BALANCE**	Over-Protecting Under-Accepting	Destructively Over-Protecting Under-Accepting	
PLEASERS			DEFENDERS		
Exploited Checked out Codependent Resentful Weak	Complacent People pleasing Capitulating Martyr Passive	Clear Reasonable Kind Courageous Satisfied	Controlling Intolerant Smug Critical Rigid	Aggressive Punitive Contentious Abandoning Manipulating	
SELF-DESTRUCTIVE	SELF-DEPRIVING	SELF-RESPECTING	SELF-RIGHTEOUS	SELF-CENTERED	

The mistake I made in those early years was that I failed to acknowledge my disappointment before trying to be more accepting. Whenever September was late, I would tell myself, "I'm clearly not important to my wife," or "She only cares about herself and her own agenda," which fueled my overreacting. I didn't stop to give voice to these assumptions, so I could not check if they were true. Often I was not reacting to her being late, but to her being selfish and rude (my interpretation), which gave me permission to overreact, either by expressing anger when she arrived or by fuming in pouty silence.

These ongoing skirmishes were harming our relationship, and something had to change. I began listening to her critique of my over-reactions and realized they sounded surprisingly similar to critiques I sometimes received from others. My contribution to our repeated conflicts had been a blind spot for me. And once I recognized that blind spot, I could see my overreactions were widening the gap with my wife and making things worse. The prospect of being the one narrowing the gap instead of widening it motivated me to change. While I couldn't change September's lateness habit, I could change me. Today, although I certainly don't bat a thousand in this area, I've made dramatic improvements.

But even if September didn't change a bit, the change in *me* would have narrowed our gap. I'm not suggesting that the best response to someone who is chronically late is always to be primarily accepting, or that every situation will end better for both parties. There are circumstances around punctuality where a little protecting is in order. But in the case of September's punctuality, I was over-protecting.

These days, when I want to acknowledge my disappointment about September's lateness, I first try to hear her out so I can calibrate my hurt appropriately. Here's how a late-for-lunch conversation might go today:

> **Me:** Thanks for meeting me for lunch. But I was expecting you to be here twenty minutes ago, at noon. Am I missing something?
>
> **September:** Really? I had 12:30 p.m. on my calendar. *Or,* You're right, but I lost my keys and got a late start. Sorry for making you wait. I should have called.

If September said simply, "Yeah, sorry I'm late," without explanation or genuine levels of remorse or ownership, then it might be time to consider a shift from primarily accepting to more protecting.

In either of these cases, hearing September's response helps me right-size my level of disappointment. I can avoid over-protecting and respond in a way that matches reality. No matter how the other person responds, you'll know you've done your part by first right-sizing your disappointment before you respond.

Another benefit of giving voice to your disappointment is to determine whether you and the other person are aligned on the issue. In the previous hypothetical scenario, if my wife were a mere three minutes late and I gave voice to my disappointment, she may respond, "When I am coming from across town, I don't consider three minutes to be late. I would hope that you'd offer me more leeway than three minutes before you become disappointed."

In this case, by giving voice to my disappointment, my wife and I can recalibrate what we consider to be reasonable expectations of each other. I might recognize that my disappointment was not reasonable and adjust accordingly. But if I had not given voice to my disappointment and discussed it with September, I would continue to feel unreasonably slighted whenever she was three minutes late. Left unchecked, the gap between us would have grown wider.

Naming Your Disappointment Honors
Your Voice, Desires, and Dignity

Another benefit of naming our disappointment is that it helps us be honest about how we're feeling. We've right-sized our expectations and recognized we have a right to be hurt. Too often, however, we respond with silence. We say nothing. But the problem with saying nothing is that, when we let our silence communicate for us, we have no control over what we say. The person who has disappointed us can take any number of messages from our silence, the most likely being, "No problem here!" By remaining silent, we're more likely to experience recurring disappointments.

When you give voice to your disappointment, you have control over what you communicate. You can let

> THE PROBLEM WITH SAYING NOTHING IS THAT, WHEN WE LET OUR SILENCE COMMUNICATE FOR US, WE HAVE NO CONTROL OVER WHAT WE SAY.

the person know that while you're not devastated, you're not thrilled either, or that you have feelings worth listening to.

Ignoring the problem by remaining silent isn't the same as accepting. When you name your disappointment, you grow in the skill of self-advocacy, and the other person grows in their understanding of how their choices affect you. Their respect for you may grow as well: you're no pushover, you have opinions, and you're reasonable and kind. By your silence the other person may assume that your needs aren't important. So by giving voice to your disappointment, you kindly but clearly reaffirm that your needs and desires deserve consideration. It's a win-win.

In the earlier late-for-lunch example, when I gave voice to my disappointment, my conversation with my wife accomplished more than just right-sizing or validating my interpretation of the situation, it also communicated to September that being twenty minutes late isn't ideal. This reaffirms the value of treating one another with respect, and makes it easier for me to know how to react if she's late in the future.

When giving voice to your disappointments, your tone of voice and choice of words make all the difference. Acknowledging your disappointment in a kind manner allows you to sincerely build a bridge toward the other person while keeping the conversation rooted in truth, respect, and dignity. If you make a habit of starting your conversation with a curious, kind, and heartfelt tone and facial expression, you develop a natural rhythm of communicating and recalibrating your disappointments without making a big deal or making the other person feel defensive. This is always a challenge for me, but it's a game changer—particularly for us protectors.

Imagine my wife walked into the restaurant twenty minutes late and I greeted her with an eye roll and a sarcastic, "Thanks for making me wait!" or an accusatory, "Why are you *always* late?!" Such responses would have put her on the defensive. I would have sabotaged any chance of building a bridge toward her and would have certainly widened our relational gap.

Acknowledging your disappointment isn't a hard-and-fast rule. Clearly there are times when you feel disappointed but the wisest thing to do is to keep quiet. September and I recently attended a dinner prepared by a new and dear friend, Jane. She asked ahead of time what kind of food we liked, and we shared that we love Mexican food. In response, she announced that she'd make enchiladas—and I was excited.

When we arrived, it was obvious that Jane had worked hard to prepare a fantastic meal and was hoping for our approval. Unfortunately for me, her enchilada masterpiece was packed with onions, the one ingredient on the planet that I find nearly intolerable. I was disappointed. (September, however, was thrilled because she loves onions but refrains from cooking with them because of my aversion.) Obviously, at that moment, it would have been unkind to give voice to my unmet desire for onion-free enchiladas, and so I kept quiet. Fortunately, even with the onions, the enchiladas were delicious, and the evening was delightful.

To have given voice to my disappointment during our first meal together would have been unkind. But as we have gotten closer, I shared with Jane my odd but strong quirk for "no-onion zone" cooking. She promised an onion-free meal next time.

The art of knowing when it's wise and when it's unwise to give voice to our disappointments is a skill that requires discernment, and we develop it with practice. Imagine you have a monthly breakfast with a close friend, and every time you get together, he shows you a dozen pictures of his grandchildren. You think, as I would, *Seriously? Not again. How much could these kids possibly have changed in thirty days? Please don't make me look at more pictures!* But he is so proud of his grandkids, and it means a lot to him to share his joy with you. In this situation, you might choose not to give voice to your disappointment and decide to just "oooh" and "ahhh" over his grandkids. It only costs you five minutes a month but means so much to him. The violation of your desires and expectations is small, and there is no risk to your sense of value, safety, or dignity; therefore, it's not worth hurting your friend's feelings.

But what if you have a friend who works for you, and she consistently pulls out her photos during your weekly staff meeting. In this situation, the proud-grandma tour has a greater cost to you. It's taking away valuable work time and sending the wrong message to your other team members about the purpose of a work meeting. Therefore, it would be reasonable—in fact, necessary—to take her aside and remind her that weekly staff meetings aren't an appropriate place for sharing family photos. With a kind tone of voice, carefully chosen words, and affirming body language, you can communicate your desire that she cease and desist the weekly photo displays in a way that minimizes hurt feelings.

If you are an acceptor, you might be tempted to use the point of this last section as permission to accept without giving voice to your disappointment. But the times when you *won't* need to give voice are rare. Don't succumb to this mistake.

2. Don't Make a Big Deal About It

The second task of a primarily accepting response in the "During" stage is to not make a big deal. Just because you're disappointed or unhappy doesn't mean that life is terrible, that something must change, or that someone must be proven wrong. Even when your feelings of disappointment are reasonable, once you've given appropriate voice to your missed desire, it may be best to build a bridge toward the other person by not making a big deal about your disappointment.

Disappointments are a normal part of life, and they help me to remember that I cause my own fair share of disappointments for others. This truth alone helps me resist the temptation to make a big deal over a small disappointment.

So what does "not making a big deal about something" look like? Great question. Here's my advice: the best way to not make a big deal about something is to not make a big deal about something. It's not a whole lot more complicated than that. But it's worth going a little deeper than my profound words of wisdom.

When we feel a little disappointed or we get slighted by a small infraction, but the infraction hasn't created enough of a gap to require protecting ourselves, the battle becomes an internal one. We must reconcile the tension between our disappointment and our sense that it's best not to make a big deal out of it. We must actively resist the inner tendency to catastrophize or to tell distorted stories about the situation that would justify an overreaction. This part of accepting is hard for me because I tend to be hypervigilant and a little paranoid about protecting myself from slights. When I'm hurt, I try to convince myself that the other person, or what they did to me, is worse than they really are to justify my over-protection.

Here is the key: the first few seconds matter. For me, success hinges on how I respond in those moments immediately after I feel slighted. If I discipline myself not to react or assume the worst of the other person in those first seconds, I can usually grab the reins of my emotions, take a deep breath, and then process the situation in a more rational and accurate manner. If you're a protector, the first piece of action is to not react immediately. Take time to assess. In these circumstances, I appreciate this encouragement from the apostle Paul to his friends in Ephesus:

> Be completely humble and gentle; be patient, bearing with one another in love. Make every effort to keep the unity of the Spirit through the bond of peace. (Eph. 4:2–3)

After Your Response

Let It Go

Okay, so you've recognized that you were disappointed, and you've discerned that the most productive response was to be primarily accepting. You gently gave voice to your frustration, and then you chose not to make a big deal about it. Great work.

Now comes the tricky part: actually letting it go. Sometimes we succeed in not making a big deal on the outside, but just can't seem to get over it on the inside. The hurt still lingers. We keep circling back to it in our thoughts. It eats away at us, and we hold a grudge. When we find ourselves unable to let go and move on, it generally means that we're still making it a big deal at some level, even if the other person is unaware.

This is the hard part for me. When I get to this step of accepting, I nearly always need to spend focused time dedicated to truly letting things go during my morning meditation. During those times I sit with a quote from the book of Proverbs: "A person's wisdom yields patience; it is to one's glory to overlook an offense" (19:11).

Not making a big deal about something isn't the same thing as letting go. Sometimes we refrain from making a big deal but still harbor resentment. Or, we choose to not make a big deal by simply stuffing our hurt and continuing in our relationship. When we do this, the disappointment becomes our constant companion throughout the relationship, often leading to resentment and bitterness. Also, if we're still holding on to our disappointment on the inside, we'll be tempted to use the infraction as ammunition during future discussions or arguments.

When we succeed at not making a big deal of the issue, we release the other person from further consequences for the infraction, and we don't act like martyrs or heroes for doing so. We don't behave as if the other person now owes us because we were so accepting. Letting go means letting go. No strings attached. No unpaid debt. No lingering score to be settled. We're able to move on with a clean slate.

Some of us experience situations

NOT MAKING A BIG DEAL ABOUT SOMETHING ISN'T THE SAME THING AS LETTING GO.

where we just can't let the issue go, even though we know in our hearts that it would be the best thing to do for all involved. If the hurt you're feeling is at the hand of someone in your life with whom you feel safe, then having a candid and vulnerable conversation with that person before reacting will often bring clarity. For example, because I'm an over-protector, I often find myself feeling slighted or hurt, and then I wonder if this is one of those times when I'm overreacting. Sometimes I go to my wife or my boss or a close friend and ask something like:

- "Can I check in with you on something? I've been playing our last interaction back in my head, and I'm left with some questions."
- "I could very well be misinterpreting this situation, in which case I would love some reassurance."
- "I'm telling myself a story about us that has left me feeling hurt. Can I walk you through my experience and ask you to correct any parts that I may be missing?"

When we give it our best shot to engage in these types of conversations but feel truly unable to move on, often we find that at the root of being stuck is an issue around family of origin, forgiveness, or our own feelings of shame. While it transcends the scope of this book to go into more detail, I will say that in those circumstances, it's often well worth the time and expense to enlist the aid of a licensed therapist. Being stuck is no fun—and life has more to offer once we let go and move on.

A Story from the Home Front: The Leaky Pipe

Strengthening my ability to be primarily accepting whenever possible has proven particularly useful for me as a husband. My laid-back wife lives in the moment. As such, she gets distracted easily. The phrase she often uses to describe her occasional lack of focus is, "Oops! I saw something shiny." If she sees a need in the moment, that "shiny thing" grabs her attention, and she quickly switches track to attend to it. Her propensity to respond to shiny things is usually beneficial to those she loves; my needs and those of the kids are often her "shiny" things. However, she sometimes forgets what she was in the middle of doing before she spotted the shiny thing, which can be at times problematic.

I remember once when September and I were working on a leaking pipe in the sump pump of our basement. Water was spraying all over the cement wall, so I wrapped my hands around the leaking joint and asked September to run up to the garage and get my pipe wrench. Two minutes went by, then three, then five. I hollered for her, but she was out of earshot. *Dang. She saw something shiny.* I was disappointed. My hands were freezing from the icy water, and now I had to go fetch the tool myself, allowing water to spray everywhere until I returned.

In our earlier years of marriage, I would take an oversight like this personally. I'd feel slighted and then get angry. But I have since realized that when these things happen, September means no harm. Her propensity for shiny things can be frustrating at times, but it's also what the kids and I love best about her: joyful spontaneity and willingness to drop everything to help someone, even if she was in the midst of helping someone else. I could feel disappointed and even frustrated that I had been left stranded and needed to let more water leak while I retrieved my wayward spouse and the pipe wrench, but anger here would be unwarranted.

I went upstairs, and there was my wife sitting at the kitchen table, helping one of our kids with a college application. As soon as September saw me, she remembered her wayward task, and her face turned white.

"Agh! The pipe wrench!" she said. "I'm so sorry!" She stood to head to the garage.

I grinned and shook my head. (I may even have pressed my wet, freezing cold fingers against her cheeks.) Because I had reacted with a primarily accepting response rather than my more natural tendency to be primarily protecting, we laughed about it, and I let it go.

Whenever September is forgetful or late, I try to remind myself of the positive side of her easygoing nature and how much I gain from living with her light and relaxed temperament. I'm usually able to coach myself: "September's late. My tendency is to take this personally, but in all likelihood something important or unavoidable came up, or she just got sidetracked. It's frustrating when she's late, but I actually like the laid-back part of her, so I don't need to make a big deal." This kind of self-talk helps keep my internal energy from ramping up out of proportion to the infraction. I can then employ a primarily accepting response and not make a big deal.

Similarly, September has learned to right-size my intense personality. If we're deep in conversation and I speak in a tone that's a little too blunt, she tries to remind herself that I tend to cut to the chase and speak in absolutes. These more abrasive parts of me are part of my diagnostic approach to problems—strengths she tells me she appreciates. If my words or tone are too sharp, she gives voice to her frustration, and I apologize. She also reminds herself that my goal isn't to hurt her feelings but to be helpful, and that she usually benefits from my diagnostic, decisive nature. This allows her to find that ideal balance between giving voice to her disappointment and not making a big deal. She'll then let it go, which I greatly appreciate.

We both recognize that we gain balance from the other's personality. She gains from my clarity and directness, and I gain from her easygoing nature, making it easier to give the other the benefit of the doubt and not over-protect or over-accept.

If my blunt words or September's lateness escalates into a recurring *pattern*, or if our behavior toward the other person is demeaning, aggressive, or damaging, then a response of primarily accepting would be the wrong choice. Those aren't times to build a bridge; instead, they're times to protect. This is the topic of the next chapter.

FOUR

Protecting: When Boundary Setting Is the Ideal Strategy

WHERE WE'RE HEADED:

- What a boundary is
- What a boundary is *not*

What about those times when the right thing to do is to make a big deal?

If someone's actions or ongoing patterns of behavior put our safety, value, or dignity at risk, it's time to make a big deal. If we don't infuse some protection into the situation, things will only get worse. Status quo means the relationship will continue to deteriorate until it becomes an endurance test, oozes into an unsatisfying coexistence, or escalates into an abuser/abused battle zone.

This does not mean that we protect ourselves only when the infraction is enormous. All disappointments deserve careful navigation. Sometimes the problems are ongoing and involve small but destructive patterns of behavior. We're more prone to ignore long-standing, mildly destructive patterns because each incident by itself is no big deal. It's the accumulation of incidents that creates a need for protection. Such patterns are sometimes harder to identify than big infractions because they creep up on us.

If Your Disappointment Is Minor but Ongoing

In times when your disappointment is minor, but your previous attempts to react with a primarily accepting response have not resulted in shifting a pattern, you will likely need to increase your level of protecting. For example, if you and your spouse disagree about what to watch on TV one night, you can start with a primarily accepting position and let your spouse choose the show. But if your spouse has been the TV-show chooser for the last fifteen nights in a row, now you're facing a pattern that's unfair.

WHEN THE STRATEGY OF PRIMARILY ACCEPTING FAILS TO RESTORE YOUR SAFETY, VALUE, OR DIGNITY, OR THAT OF ANOTHER PERSON, YOU MUST SHIFT YOUR STRATEGY BY DECREASING THE LEVEL OF ACCEPTING YOU OFFER AND INCREASING THE LEVEL OF PROTECTING.

Even though the issue is small, its ongoing nature may jeopardize your sense of value or dignity, which signals that it's time to set a boundary. Remember, achieving the balance between accepting and protecting is not an either/or scenario; it's readjusting the mixture of those two ingredients to make the relationship function well. When the strategy of primarily accepting fails to restore your safety, value, or dignity, or that of another person, you must shift your strategy by decreasing the level of accepting you offer and increasing the level of protecting.

Both building a bridge and setting a boundary share a common goal: to create a healthier relationship. The difference is in the strategy and how that strategy gets played out.

WHAT IS SETTING A BOUNDARY?

"Good fences make good neighbors," wrote Robert Frost.[1] In this famous poem, each spring a neighbor insists on working with Frost to repair a stone fence that separates their properties, so there will be no lack of clarity on where one person's property ends and another person's property begins. That's a pretty good illustration of setting a boundary.

The term *boundary*, in a relational sense, gained broad usage after the release of the bestseller, *Boundaries: When to Say Yes, How to Say No to Take Control of Your Life* by Henry Cloud and John Townsend in 1992. (If you've not yet read this classic work on boundaries, I highly recommend it.) For our purposes, setting boundaries is defined as follows: keeping the adverse consequences of someone's choices or behavior with their rightful owner.

Let's use the analogy of a garden to get clarity on when setting a boundary is appropriate. Imagine I have a garden that I protect with a small fence, which is next to your garden that you protect with a similar fence. The vegetables I choose to grow and how often I choose to weed my garden are my prerogative. Similarly, the vegetables you choose to grow and how often you choose to weed

> FOR OUR PURPOSES, SETTING BOUNDARIES IS DEFINED AS FOLLOWS: KEEPING THE ADVERSE CONSEQUENCES OF SOMEONE'S CHOICES OR BEHAVIOR WITH THEIR RIGHTFUL OWNER.

your garden are up to you. If I try to tell you how to manage your garden, you can gently remind me that my area of responsibility is on my side of the fence. If I still insist on getting involved in your gardening choices despite your reminder, you may need to use a stronger voice or build a bigger fence.

Let's pretend that you're an attentive gardener who weeds and waters regularly. I, on the other hand, let weeds run wild, blowing dreaded dandelion seeds onto your carefully weeded plot. I also allow my sprinkler to flood your garden, eroding your soil and waterlogging your plants. The consequences of how I choose to garden are now adversely impacting your garden. What should you do?

If you've voiced your disappointment to me but nothing changes, you have every right to protect yourself from these adverse consequences by building a tall, solid fence that keeps *my* weeds and *my* water in *my* garden. (Realistically, you and I both know that no fence on earth will stop dandelions. Remember, this is a pretend scenario.)

Setting boundaries keeps adverse consequences with their rightful owner. This definition of setting boundaries provides clarity on the challenges we face when navigating a relational gap. But who is the rightful owner of which consequence? In the heat of battle, getting clear on who owns which consequence is sometimes hard to discern.

Imagine you have a coworker who procrastinates on her projects and routinely comes to you for help when a project is already near or past the deadline. You dive in and rescue her, but in the process your own projects fall behind. You're frustrated, and you recognize that up to this point you've been over-accepting. It's time to increase the proportion of protecting by setting a boundary—but who will be the owner of which consequence?

In this scenario, your coworker's procrastination produces the negative consequence of her projects not getting completed on time without your help, and she responds to her negative consequence by asking you to rescue her at the last minute. The boundary you need to set must ensure that she keeps the consequences of her lack of planning and needing help at the last minute in her lap, not yours. She's the rightful owner of those consequences.

Here is the tricky part: *you* are the owner of any consequences that come from having waited so long to set a boundary; you're the owner of your frustration and resentment; and you're the owner of your projects falling behind. These are the negative consequences from your pattern of being over-accepting with your coworker until now.

The list below offers some examples of who owns which consequence in different relational scenarios:

OTHERS ARE THE RIGHTFUL OWNERS OF CONSEQUENCES FROM THEIR . . .	YOU ARE THE RIGHTFUL OWNER OF CONSEQUENCES FROM YOUR . . .
poor choices	tendency to rescue others after poor choices
unresolved family-of-origin issues	fear and guilt around setting boundaries due to family-of-origin issues
not telling the truth	ignoring the other's pattern of lying
not planning ahead	saying yes, even though doing so creates significant hardship
behaviors that lead to lost jobs	tendency to control through "helping"
not having enough money	not setting limits
anger when someone sets boundaries	backing down when someone responds with anger

When responding to our gaps with increased levels of protecting, we must make sure we're addressing the consequences of the other person's behavior, and not our reactions to their behavior. For example, you have a friend who keeps getting fired from jobs because of his unreliability. He then has a pattern of asking you for a "loan" for gas, which you keep giving. But then you feel resentful because he never pays you back.

In this scenario, who is the rightful owner of which consequence? Your friend is the rightful owner of the consequence of not being able to hold a job, and thus not having gas money. And you're the rightful owner of the consequences of enabling your friend with ongoing loans that are never repaid, as well as your shrinking bank account and your growing resentment.

Keeping consequences with their rightful owner clarifies the situation and helps you avoid storing up anger, hurt, or resentment. When your unemployed friend asks for another loan, you can say no, not because of your mounting anger and resentment, but because you recognize you have been inappropriately carrying the consequences of *his* not keeping a job—consequences of which *he* is the rightful owner, not you.

In saying no, you might worry about your friend, or even be fearful of being rejected, but you won't feel resentful. You'll be less likely to let anger build up inside you. And you can sympathize with your friend's plight without enabling his inability to hold a job. He will feel the natural consequences of whatever keeps him from remaining gainfully employed. Perhaps this will motivate him to solve the root problem. But even if he never learns to be a responsible employee, you can choose to maintain your friendship guilt- and resentment-free.

Since boundaries are often set when we're no longer willing to own the consequences that belong to someone else, the shift in strategy from accepting to protecting is by definition a defensive maneuver. A good defense helps prevent harm at the hand of another person. A true boundary doesn't ask, expect, or demand the other person change their behavior; it is a purely defensive tool. It simply places the consequences of that person's behavior back into their lap where they belong, rather than keeping them in your lap.

We can only manage what we can control: our own responses and behaviors. We cannot control the behaviors of others. Therefore, when setting a boundary, we don't tell the other person what to do or what not to do. We simply describe to them how *we* will respond to their behavior, moving forward. In the previous example, if you adopt a more protecting response and set a boundary with your friend, you're not telling him to get a job or to stop asking for money, you're simply letting him know that you'll no longer loan him money. Setting this boundary is a protecting, defensive move, not a reactionary, offensive move.

In my experience, when people struggle with setting boundaries, the problem usually isn't with their inability to set a boundary, it's with their misunderstanding of what a boundary actually is. One of the simplest ways to answer the question, What is a boundary? is to get clear on what a boundary is *not*.

What a Boundary Is *Not*

Many times in my office, after hearing a difficult relational story, I suggest, "Perhaps it's time to set a boundary," I'm often met with some common forms of resistance:

- "I already tried setting a boundary, and it didn't work."
- "They kept right on lying [or using drugs, demeaning me, yelling at me at work, etc.]."
- "It just made things worse."
- "They won't respect my boundaries."

In most situations, the problem is not that their boundaries didn't work, but that the person setting the boundary is confused about what a boundary is and what it is not. There are three common misunderstandings about boundaries. Boundaries are *not*:

1. A tool to coerce, manipulate, or change the other person
2. A weapon to hurt the other person, seek justice, or exact revenge
3. An excuse to abandon or escape from a relationship

Let's examine each of these misconceptions more closely.

1. Boundaries Are *Not* a Tool to Coerce, Manipulate, or Change the Other Person

It's okay to *desire* that someone change their unhealthy patterns. If the other person's behavior is self-destructive and we care about them, it's natural that we'd want them to make different choices. If that person's behavior hurts us or others we care about, of course we'd want them to stop. What's not okay is to *expect* or *demand* that they change their behavior. We can only change our own behavior. Remember, boundaries are about defense, not offense.

Let's revisit the analogy of fences to understand this concept. My wife, an avid gardener, experienced firsthand the importance of adequate fences as a defensive tool last summer.

Each spring, September spends a great deal of time planting, watering, weeding, and feeding a vast variety of fruits and vegetables in our backyard. She orders heirloom seeds online, plants them indoors, transplants her homegrown seedlings into the garden, installs watering systems, and tends to her raised beds and containers with near-obsessive vigor. Her garden is an investment and a beloved part of her life, over which she is understandably protective.

But last summer, when our family should have been basking in the (literal) fruits of her labor, she noticed that her tomatoes and berries were disappearing. Then one morning she discovered that something had dug huge pits in her small corn patch and destroyed several stalks of corn overnight. So I wired up a motion-detecting floodlight and aimed it at the garden. That night around 2:00 a.m., the light flicked on, illuminating our backyard and our bedroom. I awoke and peeked out of our bedroom window but saw nothing. I then sneaked out onto our back deck, flashlight in hand. Hearing a rustling noise below, I aimed my flashlight at the garden just in time to see not one, not two, not three, but *four* well-fed raccoons scurrying from the scene of the crime.

September was incensed. All her hours of preparation, seedling care, and transplanting were being destroyed by these masked bandits. She decided to take action. Her first pass at defending her garden involved a rigorous strategy of netting and setting physical barriers, which merely gave the raccoons a little chuckle when they returned the next night; they continued pillaging her garden with minimal delay.

September realized she had to raise the stakes in her raccoon-warfare tactics, so she went electric. September and I grew up in the country, and we were familiar with the harmless but startling effects of low-voltage electric fencing. My dad used these fences all over our property to keep cows and horses within their corrals. Although I was less familiar with using them on smaller animals, with some trial and error, I hooked up the garden expanse with a mild electric fence designed for pets; that is, two strands of wire placed low to the ground.

And then we waited.

In the wee hours that night, our motion light came on. We lay in bed listening. And sure enough, within a few seconds, we heard the angry yelps of our surprised and disappointed tribe of raccoons. We high-fived each other and went back to sleep, knowing September's territory was adequately protected. The next night the same routine happened: floodlight came on, followed by what I can only assume was an angry string of raccoon curse words and hand gestures, then the sound of scurrying feet as the masked villains left in defeat. September's corn, tomatoes, and berries were safe.

The motion light came on periodically throughout that summer, and when I peeked outside I'd see the raccoons hanging around in our backyard looking for stray apples under the apple tree or digging for grubs near the fence. But they had learned to stay clear of the garden. Once in a while, a raccoon, perhaps new to the neighborhood or just a slow learner, would test the boundary and receive our low-volt shock treatment. (Cue raccoon cursing.) The protective and defensive boundary worked; the critters stayed out of her garden.

Now imagine if September were to complain, "But the raccoons are still in our yard, and they're staring at our veggies! Plus, they're probably stealing from our neighbor's garden. The fence failed." She would have missed the whole point of the boundary. The sole sign of success for this electric fence is that her vegetables remain untouched by the raccoons.

Good boundaries don't remove the raccoons, keep them from coming around at night to admire her veggies, stop them from stealing veggies from other peoples' gardens, or convince them to take up gardening and plant their own tomatoes and corn. The boundary wasn't put in place to reform the raccoons but to defend what September has the right to control: her garden.

If, as a result of September's boundary, the raccoons choose to stop *attempting* to steal, that would be fantastic. But that's not the goal of a boundary; the goal is to stop the actual stealing. Because September placed an effective, defensive boundary—the electric fence—the consequences of their attempting to steal are placed squarely on the raccoons themselves. Remember, boundaries are for defense, not offense. They don't dictate the behavior of someone else; they simply keep that behavior from adversely affecting you.

[BOUNDARIES] DON'T DICTATE THE BEHAVIOR OF SOMEONE ELSE; THEY SIMPLY KEEP THAT BEHAVIOR FROM ADVERSELY AFFECTING YOU.

The most common and costly mistake we make when setting a boundary is trying to use the boundary to change the other person's behavior. Just as September cannot reform the raccoons, we cannot reform other people. But we have the right to control our own property, choices, and behavior—everything that is rightfully ours.

Sometimes in our relationships we have conversations with those close to us in hopes of influencing their behavior or choices. For example, we ask our spouse to keep their spending within our agreed-upon budget, our college-bound children not to abuse alcohol, or our bosses not to verbally abuse us. These requests make sense. They're perfectly wise and reasonable. But let's be clear, these conversations are not boundary discussions.

A boundary dictates only how we will behave, not how the other person will behave. We can choose to respond to the destructive behavior of others in a new way moving forward, but we cannot dictate better behavior from other people. A boundary simply keeps the consequences of bad behavior with their rightful owner; it protects when accepting will no longer suffice.

A Story of Jake and His Wife

Jake came to my office to talk about some problems he was having with his wife. But he reacted with considerable energy when I suggested that it may be time to set a boundary in response to his wife's significant alcohol abuse.

"Boundaries are worthless!" he said. "I tried setting boundaries with her, but she's still drinking."

He confused boundaries with control. Boundaries would keep the adverse consequences of his wife's drinking with their rightful owner: his wife. Control would make his wife stop drinking, something only Jake's wife has the power to do.

When you set a true boundary designed to protect yourself, it may or may not motivate the other person to change their behavior. But changing someone else isn't your goal. You can only change yourself. Jake's wife *may* choose to stop drinking once he stops bearing the natural consequences of her alcohol abuse and allows her to experience the full consequences of her drinking. If his boundary prompts his wife to get help, that's great. But that result is out of his control. Only his wife can control her drinking.

Regardless of how his wife responds, Jake can control his own responses to her alcohol abuse. He may choose to leave the Christmas party as soon as his wife becomes tipsy and let her take a cab home, alone. He can stop covering for her at work when she's hung over. He may need to separate their finances if he's unable to protect his earnings from her alcohol abuse and the resulting legal expenses of her driving under the influence. If he or their kids are at risk, he may need to ask her to move out or seek a legal separation.

None of these boundaries will be easy. But setting them is his only hope for getting free of the consequences of his wife's choices. Nagging his wife to stop drinking not only doesn't work, it only adds to their mutual disappointment, and distracts Jake from strategies that would protect him from the consequences of her alcohol abuse. By setting defensive boundaries with her, he can find dignity, protection, and peace for himself and their kids—regardless of how his wife chooses to respond.

A Story of Suzanne and Her Son, Ryan

In my office I had the following exchange with Suzanne, a woman troubled by her adult son's use of marijuana:

> **Suzanne:** I tried setting boundaries with Ryan, but it didn't work. I told him that as long as he's smoking pot, I will no longer send him money to help cover his living expenses in New York City. I don't want him using my money to buy pot. He kept smoking, so I stopped paying. But despite that boundary, he still is using pot.
>
> **Me:** I'm sorry to hear that. But it sounds like you're not really setting a boundary with Ryan. It sounds more like you're trying to coerce him into not smoking pot.

Suzanne: But I used the kind of language that the books suggest: "If you choose to continue to smoke marijuana, I will no longer pay for your cell phone."

Me: That's great. Your decision to stop inadvertently funding his drug habit is a fine idea. But what's your motive? What do you *really* want?

Suzanne: I want him to stop using drugs.

Me: That's a reasonable desire. I'd want the same thing. But when it comes to his drug use, how does that affect you directly? In other words, what adverse consequence of his pot smoking are *you* carrying?

Suzanne: Well, for one thing, I worry. I'm afraid for his future. I fear something bad will happen to him, given the type of people he's hanging out with. And, to be honest, I'm embarrassed that I have a son who's a drug user.

Me: What happens when you get worried or embarrassed?

Suzanne: I try to talk some sense into him. But he's twenty-three years old, so it's not like he has to do what I say. I usually end up losing my temper or bursting into tears. I'm just at a loss for how to fix this.

Me: All those things make sense. I'm so sorry you're in this situation. Will you humor me with one more question?

Suzanne: Okay . . .

Me: Who is the rightful owner of your fear for Ryan's well-being and your embarrassment over his drug use?

Suzanne paused, and then her eyes filled with tears.

Suzanne: I guess I'm the rightful owner. I mean, his pot smoking triggers my fear, because I love him and care what happens to him. But I'm probably the one who should own my emotions. Still, don't you think it's reasonable that I want my son not to use drugs?

Me: Absolutely! But if you're the rightful owner of your own feelings of fear and embarrassment, then it's probably unfair for Ryan to be on the receiving end of the consequences of your feelings when you lay into him about his drug use.

Suzanne paused again, and then reached for a tissue.

Suzanne: It's just so hard to watch him self-destruct.

Me: No doubt. I'd feel the same way if I were in your shoes. And it's totally reasonable to talk with your son about his pot smoking and invite him to make different choices. That's good parental coaching. But that isn't setting a boundary. It sounds like your motivation in withholding money is to change his behavior.

Suzanne: So do you think that I should just continue to fund his drug habit?!

Me: Of course not. I really like your boundary of not funding his behaviors. I would just argue that your boundary was actually a success: no more of your money is being redirected to help your son pay for an illegal substance. Remember, your goal is to keep consequences with their rightful owner. You're no longer carrying the financial consequences of Ryan's choices. And you're sparing him from carrying the consequences of your worry.

Suzanne: But what if he gets arrested?!

Me: That would be sad. But he's an adult. That would be a predictable consequence of his adult choices. He'll need to figure that out for himself.

Suzanne: I would feel so sad.

Me: And that's a sign that your boundaries are working. Your anger and fear are being replaced by the emotion of deep sadness. Boundaries won't take that part away. But they can leave you with a sense of peace, knowing you're doing everything you can to have a healthy relationship with your son.

Suzanne was using a boundary (withholding her money) as a means to coerce her son and get something she wanted from him (that he stop using drugs). She expected this boundary to control him, and to protect his future and her reputation. Even though the boundary was technically successful in that she no longer carried the negative consequence of her money being diverted toward illegal substances, she interpreted the boundary as a failure, and so her anger and resentment toward Ryan grew.

Ironically, her angry reaction to his drug use only heightened Ryan's anxiety and increased his usage. Suzanne's misunderstanding of boundaries actually got her the opposite of what she wanted. Once she was able to right-size her expectations of that boundary and unhook herself from her son's choices, after an initial rise in tension, their relationship improved dramatically. Eventually, Ryan chose to get help for his abuse of pot. But even if he had not, Suzanne had learned how to be in a relationship with her adult son without trying to control his behavior.

A Story from the Home Front: Pouting

In the earlier years of my marriage, I would often resort to pouting when in conflict with my wife. September would do something that hurt my feelings, and rather than having an honest conversation about what happened, I would withdraw and sulk. When she asked if something was wrong, I would self-righteously declare that I was too hurt to talk about it so I was setting a boundary and withdrawing.

Obviously, this was not setting a boundary; it was manipulation. I was trying to coerce my wife into begging me to tell her how she had hurt me and pursue me to make things right. Although there are times when withdrawal in a relationship is a reasonable boundary to set, in my case, I was stonewalling, not setting a boundary. I was using withdrawal as a tool to coerce my wife into doing what I wanted.

To discern if your motivation to set a boundary is being skewed by your desire to change the other person, ask yourself: What consequence am I carrying in this situation of which I am *not* the rightful owner?

A Story from Concerned Family Members

I am sometimes approached by people looking for help with setting a boundary on adult family members because their loved ones are "wasting their life away," "not raising their children in a responsible manner," or any number of similar complaints. I was once approached by John, a man who wanted to set a boundary with his son and daughter-in-law, and our conversation went something like this:

> **John:** I need to set a boundary with my son and his wife. They just let their kids watch TV all day and eat junk food. It's just awful.
>
> **Me:** Wow, that sounds hard.
>
> **John:** I just can't stand it. I need to do something. It's time to set a boundary.
>
> **Me:** What negative consequence of their parenting choices are you carrying?

66

John: Well . . . my heart is broken for my grandkids, and I'm worried about their future.

Me: That sounds reasonable. Who is the owner of your heartbreak and your worry?

John: Uh . . . me?

Me: Yep.

John: So what am I supposed to do? Just stand around and watch them ruin their kids' lives?!

Me: Well, unless they all live with you, you really don't have any control in this situation. And because, at this time, you're not carrying any direct consequences of their parenting choices, you really have no boundary to set. You cannot control them. But you can earn their trust and invite dialogue.

John: Believe me, I've tried! They're not interested in any dialogue on this subject.

I feel for John and others like him. We all can probably relate to a story like this. It's a helpless feeling when an adult loved one makes poor choices. But if we're not carrying any adverse consequence from their behavior, there is no boundary to set. Our energies are best spent building our adult-to-adult relationship and hoping to invite a conversation.

In these circumstances, because you have no control, your influence must be indirect, or invited through dialogue with those you're concerned about. I'm not suggesting that you simply give up trying to influence those you love in positive ways; rather, I'm eager for you to recognize that influence isn't the same as setting a boundary. If you find you're carrying the adverse consequence of their choices or behavior, then you'll be in a trusted position to set a true boundary.

Setting Boundaries Versus Striking Bargains

In every relationship, we strike bargains; that is, if we behave a certain way, the other person may reciprocate by behaving in a certain way as well. In my marriage, September pays the bills and I keep the driveway free of snow. When we have guests over, September cooks the meal and I clear the table and do the dishes. Healthy bargains are fair to both parties, and they keep people living in harmony.

It's easy in relationships to confuse striking bargains with setting boundaries because they're both positive, helpful behaviors. But they're very different from one another: boundaries protect, bargains provide mutual rewards; boundaries keep negative consequences with their rightful owner, bargains produce positive benefits to both parties.

There are times when it makes sense to strike bargains with someone to get what we both want. We create transactional agreements, such as:

- If you will take over the laundry, I will cook the dinners.
- If you maintain a B average, I'll pay for your car insurance and phone.
- If you work an extra shift on Saturday, I will pay time-and-a-half and provide coffee and donuts.
- If you cooperate at the doctor's office while getting a shot, I will buy you an ice cream cone afterward.

Ideally, the bargain striking takes place voluntarily between trusted parties. If, after agreeing to the bargain, the other person stopped doing the laundry, got C's and D's in college, did not show up for the extra shift at work, or threw a fit at the doctor's office, they would have broken their half of the bargain and so you'd be released from upholding your half. You can't force your spouse to do laundry, your college kid to get good grades, your employee to show up for the extra shift, or your child to remain calm when it's time for their kindergarten immunizations.

Now, there may be some negative consequences from their decision to break their half of the bargain: you won't cook the dinners, pay for the car insurance, pay for the Saturday shift, or buy the ice cream. These are wise and reasonable reactions because of a broken agreement. But let's be clear, this isn't setting boundaries. Boundaries are designed for keeping consequences with their rightful owners, not for upholding a mutually beneficial agreement.

When our kids were young, September and I struck a bargain to entice them to work hard in school: if they maintained good grades, they had total control over their hairstyles. As a result, it was not uncommon in those days to see our brown-haired boys with shock-blonde buzz cuts or mohawks, or our middle school daughter with dreadlocks. This was a predetermined bargain we made, not a boundary we set.

The difference between bargaining and boundary setting is this: With bargaining, success depends on both people behaving a certain way and receiving positive rewards from the other. With boundary setting, success is measured solely by keeping consequences for people's destructive behavior with the rightful owner—them.

If it were possible to bargain with raccoons, September could have solved her garden problem by crafting a mutually rewarding transaction: "If you promise not to trash my corn, I will let each of you have a tomato every night." And if the raccoons violated the mutual agreement, she could deny them her tomatoes. But striking a bargain wasn't an option with the raccoons, so September created an electric boundary that kept the negative consequences of destructive behavior with their rightful owners: the veggie-stealing raccoons.

If you made a bargain with your son that you would pay for his cell phone plan while he was in college, and your son drops out of college, there would be an expected consequence that you'd stop paying his cell phone bill. That's not a boundary; it's simply you following through on a prearranged agreement. If your son's phone gets disconnected because he didn't pay his bill, and he requests to borrow your phone when he goes out of town for a weekend, you might choose to say no because you don't want to be without your phone. That would be a healthy boundary, because it protects you from the adverse consequence of his choosing to drop out of college.

2. Boundaries Are *Not* a Weapon to Hurt the Other Person, Seek Justice, or Exact Revenge

Too often I hear from someone who is trying to disguise their efforts to get justice or revenge as setting a boundary. It sounds something like this: "I've taken his abuse long enough! The next time he berates me in front of my coworkers, I'm going to set a boundary and give him a piece of my mind!"

In these cases, boundaries are contorted into offensive weapons. We get backed into a corner, and we're tempted to "open up a can of boundaries on him, and he won't know what hit him!" To be clear, there is nothing wrong with defending ourselves, righting wrongs, or seeking fairness. Those are all noble and important tasks. They're just not setting boundaries.

One sure indicator that we're misusing boundaries as an offensive weapon is the presence of anger. Henry Cloud captures this truth well: "Individuals with mature boundaries are the least angry people in the world."[2] We set boundaries in the hopes of preserving a relationship, not crushing it. When setting true, defensive boundaries from a healthy place, the most common emotion we'll experience isn't anger but sadness.

> ONE SURE INDICATOR THAT WE'RE MISUSING BOUNDARIES AS AN OFFENSIVE WEAPON IS THE PRESENCE OF ANGER.

A Story of Warren and Sherry

A few years back I received a meeting request from Warren, a man in his thirties from our church. A week earlier he'd discovered that his wife, Sherry, was having an affair with a guy from her work. Warren was devastated. He asked her to move out, and she was now staying with her parents. Sherry was remorseful and had already begun counseling. She had contacted the church to get help in negotiating with Warren, because he was prohibiting her from seeing their young children, ages three and one.

After spending some time listening to Warren's understandable heartbreak and offering sympathy for his situation, I shifted the topic to Sherry and the kids.

Me: Sherry contacted us for some help, because she has a deep desire to see the kids. What are your thoughts about that?

Warren: I set a boundary with Sherry. She can't see the kids until she fully owns up to the consequences of her infidelity.

Me: Your level of hurt and desire to protect the kids make sense. But I'm curious about what potential harm you see from Sherry and the kids spending time together. Do you feel she poses a risk to them?

Warren: That's not the point. She doesn't *deserve* to see the kids, because I don't think she's truly sorry for the harm she caused our marriage.

Me: Got it. Sherry's level of ownership for her affair feels like an important discussion. But first, could we sit with my original question? Does Sherry pose some kind of risk to the kids?

Warren: Well, no, not really. She's always been a really good mom. But I can't just let her go on as if nothing has happened! Shouldn't there be consequences for what she's done?

Me: Yes. She has broken trust with you as a spouse, and it would be wise for you to set some boundaries to protect your heart from further betrayal. That said, when we set a boundary the goal is to keep consequences with their rightful owner. Boundaries are for defense, not offense. Does keeping Sherry away from your kids protect either them or you in any way?

Warren: Well, no.

Me: Certainly, her breaking trust with you affects your kids at some level, since it caused deep harm to their parents' relationship. But considering their young age, do you feel Sherry violated your trust in terms of being a good mom when she's with the kids?

Warren: Probably not. She's a great mom, and my three-year-old keeps asking for her. But I know it's killing Sherry to be away from them, and to be honest, that feels sort of good right now.

Me: Makes sense. But punishing Sherry as a parent isn't the same as setting a boundary. Let's turn our focus to boundaries that actually protect you, and are a natural consequence of Sherry's behavior as a wife.

By the end of our conversation, Warren understood the difference between setting a boundary to protect himself and his children from the consequences of which Sherry was the rightful owner, and punishing his wife for her betrayal. It's not surprising that Warren had a desire to punish and control his wife after learning of her infidelity. It's human nature. But punishing and control aren't the same as setting a boundary.

An ongoing boundary may well be in order for Warren's situation. Depending on Sherry's level of sincerity in understanding her destructive choices and her willingness to make changes in her life, Warren needs to continue their separation until some trust is rebuilt between them. He deserves time to process his hurt and to heal without facing her every day at home. It wouldn't be fair of Sherry to expect him to carry the consequence of her affair (significant broken trust), while having to control his emotions in the presence of their young kids.

When we have been hurt by someone, it's tempting to confuse setting a boundary with our desire for justice. But if we give in to this temptation, we distort the gap and risk behaving in a manner that makes things worse. By keeping our focus on using boundaries as a defense move—keeping adverse consequences with their rightful owner—we take steps toward healing and growing our relationships.

3. Boundaries Are *Not* an Excuse to Abandon or Escape from a Relationship

We sometimes find ourselves in relationships that become chronically uncomfortable. Whether it's a high-maintenance sibling or a demanding longtime friend, we reach the point where we've had enough. In these situations, it makes sense to set a boundary to protect ourselves from the relational consequences that belong to the other person: their petty demands, attempts to control, overdependence, or other patterns of behavior that have become too costly to maintain. By setting boundaries that keep adverse consequences with their rightful owner, we can often break the very patterns that make those relationships unbearable. We can set new, more distant parameters that allow us to maintain the relationship with a high-maintenance sibling or a demanding friend, so that we feel less annoyed and exhausted. The relationships are then less costly to maintain.

But what if that person is unwilling to change their behavior despite our boundaries? What if we cannot escape close proximity because we're married to this person, or the person is our child or our boss? At what point do we leave a relationship altogether?

A Story of Nikki: Applying the Relational Crisis Sequence
Here's a situation I encountered with Nikki, who asked to talk with me about her marriage. She and Ralph had been married twelve years, and she was at her wit's end with their relationship.

Nikki: I finally decided to heed my friends' advice and set a boundary with Ralph, so I'm filing for divorce.

Me: Wow, that's a big decision. Which would you like to talk about first, setting a boundary or filing for divorce?

Nikki: They're the same thing! Ralph has been verbally abusive to me for our entire marriage, and I have finally had enough. I'm setting a boundary.

This was the beginning of a long and difficult conversation that exposed a sad reality: Nikki had silently endured many painful years of emotional mistreatment from Ralph, and her failure to set healthy boundaries along the way left her feeling understandably hard-hearted toward him, and hopeless that things could ever change in their relationship. She'd hit a wall, and now she just wanted out of the marriage.

Me: It makes total sense that you want to escape this painful marriage.

Nikki: Thank you! No one should expect me to endure Ralph's treatment of me.

Me: I agree. Status quo is no longer acceptable. But I'm guessing you came here today not merely to announce your decision to divorce Ralph, but to talk about it.

Nikki: I just can't take it anymore! I want out.

Me: So don't take it anymore! But my guess is, before you divorce Ralph, you want the peace of mind of knowing you did everything in your power to save the marriage.

Nikki: Yes. But I've been trying for years. I just don't know what else to do.

Me: When someone comes into this office with severe relational pain, I always suggest an important Relational Crisis Sequence:

1. Get safe.
2. Get well.
3. Then make big decisions.

Nikki: Getting divorced is definitely a big decision.

Me: While ending your marriage may be the ultimate outcome of this sequence, each step of the sequence matters, and the order of these steps especially matters. They help you make wise, healthy decisions that bring you peace of mind.

Nikki: So, by jumping to step three in the sequence before navigating steps one and two, maybe I'm jumping ahead?

Me: That would be my guess. You want to be able to stand confident of your step-three decision, knowing you gave 100 percent to steps one and two and behaved rationally, kindly, and courageously each step of the way.

Nikki: Hmm. How would I go about doing that?

Me: Great question. What do you think needs to happen for you to get safe?

Nikki: Well, Ralph has never hit me.

Me: Okay, so you're not at risk physically. But how about your emotional safety?

Nikki: At home, it's a never-ending barrage of yelling, critique, and emotional threats. I just need space. I feel like a prisoner in my own house!

Me: So how can you create emotional safety for yourself in your own home?

Nikki: I want him to move out.

Me: A separation sounds like it might be a reasonable next step, given the extreme behaviors you've described from Ralph. That would be a great topic for you and your counselor to discuss. Let's assume that you choose to separate, and for the first time in many years, you're able to catch your breath and be emotionally safe from Ralph's destructive behaviors at home. Let's look ahead to step two: get well. What would you predict will be required for you to get well?

Nikki: Me? Ralph's the one who needs to get well. He's the one with the horrible temper and the control issues! What makes you think I'm not well?

Me: Two things. First, none of us are completely well. We all have areas that need healing and growth, myself included. And second, you've willingly endured Ralph's mistreatment of you for more than a dozen years before you finally decided you couldn't take it anymore. Why didn't or couldn't you have taken a productive stand years ago? What part of you felt you deserved this kind of treatment from the one person who is supposed to value you the most?

Nikki's eyes filled. The questions about getting well led to a productive conversation about her family of origin, difficulty advocating for herself throughout her life, tendency to anesthetize her disappointments with food, and self-condemnation for her own areas of weakness.

Me: Nikki, please understand I'm not blaming you for Ralph's behavior. No one deserves to be treated this way. Instead,

I'm inviting you to be curious about your own issues over the last decade. Focusing on getting well will help you gain valuable insight into how you unwittingly contributed to the unhealthy patterns in your relationships. The "get well" step will leave you even more determined not to tolerate mistreatment from Ralph or anyone else in future relationships.

Nikki: Even before I met Ralph, I tended to date men who treated me like Ralph does. I guess there is sort of a pattern.

Me: Even if you choose to divorce Ralph, you'll want to face your future as *well* as you can be.

Nikki left my office motivated to work through the Relational Crisis Sequence (get safe, get well, then make big decisions) with her therapist before she filed for divorce.

I met with Nikki again years later. She had done great work with her therapist to better understand her contributions to the marital disharmony with Ralph. She owned her mistakes, which, granted, seemed small compared to Ralph's abusive behavior, and confessed them to her husband. Sadly, despite her sincere efforts, Ralph remained unmotivated to stop his mistreatment of her. Even after a separation, healthy boundary setting, and individual therapy, he refused to treat Nikki with respect and kindness. She eventually tackled step three of the Relational Crisis Sequence and made a big decision: she got a divorce. And because she first took time to get safe and get well, she made that difficult decision with peace and confidence.

"I'm sad we weren't able to make the marriage work," she said. "But I'm entering this next era of my life with clarity about my value as a person, a deeper understanding of who I am, and goals for where I need to grow."

Had Nikki rushed to "step 3: make big decisions" and divorced Ralph before getting safe and getting well, she would have been at significant risk for repeating the same unhealthy relational patterns in the future. But her big decision came at the end of a methodical process that required her to do substantial work on herself and take ownership for her contribution to the marital difficulty with Ralph. I hold high hopes for her future and feel confident that she can maintain healthy boundaries in any future relationships, while treating herself with dignity in the process.

The Relational Crisis Sequence works well for any distressed relationship. Whether it's an abusive boss, out-of-control adult child, manipulative parent, or selfish neighbor, the three-step process of getting safe, getting well, and then making big decisions keeps us from abandoning relationships unnecessarily. Often, once steps one and two are put in place, the big decisions that follow allow us to remain in a relationship with someone, though perhaps at a greater distance, than had we abandoned the relationship altogether.

RELATIONAL CRISIS SEQUENCE:

1. GET SAFE.

2. GET WELL.

3. THEN MAKE BIG DECISIONS.

PART II

FINDING CLARITY

WHERE WE'RE HEADED:

- Don't make things worse
- Understand your "gap" by getting clear on your desires
- Get a handle on what's really happening in the relationship

You're disappointed in a relationship and you feel some relational renovation is in order. You're convinced that you need to respond differently in the troubled relationship before things get worse. You'll either increase your amounts of accepting (build a bridge, not make a big deal, and move on) or increase your amounts of protecting (set a boundary).

In Part II, we begin working through the mechanics of the *Renovate Your Relationships Pathway* chart in detail. (See the chart on the next page.)

By far the biggest mistake we make when we're trying to decide how to respond to our relational disappointment is to fail to define the gap accurately before we attempt to manage it. Recall from chapter 1 and the "problem of life" model that our relational disappointment (the gap) is created by the chasm between what we wish were true in the relationship and what we actually experience. Our gap is the distance between our desires and our perceived reality, and the only way to get clarity on our disappointment and right-size our gaps is to examine both of these variables carefully.

Understanding how to right-size the gap is the primary task of part II. Let's begin by taking the one critical step that is essential to managing our disappointment and discerning the ideal balance of accepting and protecting.

RENOVATE YOUR RELATIONSHIPS PATHWAY

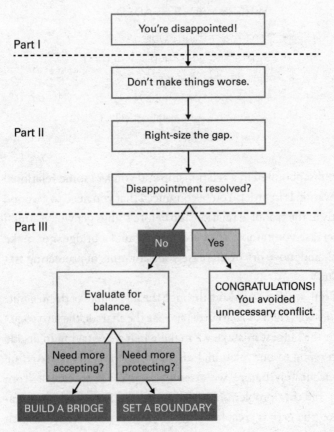

FIVE

Don't Make Things Worse

WHERE WE'RE HEADED:

- Identify your own destructive responses
- Avoid the four A's of making things worse

S igh. I reread the quote again for the third time that morning: "If it is possible, as far as it depends on you, live at peace with everyone."

Sigh. To be honest, on that particular morning, I didn't feel like living at peace with a certain individual.

This quote is one I had memorized as a college student, back when I was still an atheist but curious about spiritual things. Since then, these words have had a profound influence on my relational decisions. But even if you're not that interested in spiritual things, this quote, found in Romans 12:18 in the Bible, holds as much wisdom for you as it does for me.

One of the central themes of this book is how important it is for us to gain clarity on what we have control over and what we don't. We can only change that which we can control, and one thing is certain: we have full control over how we respond to others. Owning our responsibility for words and behaviors toward the people in our lives is a central task of living in healthy relationships.

When we're disappointed with someone, we must choose how

we'll respond. We have the opportunity and power to keep from throwing gas on the fire and fueling the problem. Our response might not make everyone happy, but we can choose to respond in a way that doesn't make things worse. We can choose words and behaviors that are productive, healing, and helpful. And we can refrain from words or behaviors that don't help or that increase the disharmony and widen the gap.

IDENTIFY YOUR OWN DESTRUCTIVE RESPONSES

I recently had a chance to hear the story of a young couple who faced relational disappointments with a parent. Their situation provides a great example of what it looks like to commit yourself to avoiding destructive responses.

Amy and Dave met on a blind date at a James Taylor concert. They dated for a couple of years, got married, and moved from the Midwest to Los Angeles for Amy's job. Two years after their marriage, their first son, Andy, was born, and they welcomed a second son, Matt, on their fifth wedding anniversary.

When Matt was born, Amy's parents, Howard and Wanda, offered to fly from Cleveland to help them with the challenge of having a newborn and a three-year-old in the house. Keenly aware of her mother's tendency to control and criticize, Amy was hesitant. But Dave thought it would be a great family-building time, so they said yes.

The first day went well, but by day two, the foundation beneath the family-building time started to crack. Wanda began her well-established pattern of picking on her daughter, both directly and indirectly. Here's a recap of their evolving dialogue:

Wanda: Where's your Windex?

Amy: Under the sink. Why?

Wanda: Because every window in this house is completely disgusting.

Amy: Mom, you're here to enjoy your grandkids. Go play outside with Andy. He's playing with the model plane you brought him. We can deal with the windows some other time.

Wanda: I would feel much better if I could actually see Andy out there, through these filthy windows.

Amy began to burn inside. This exchange was typical of how her mother has controlled and hurt her all her life. She directed Wanda to the Windex and paper towels, then disappeared into her bedroom with the baby and closed the door. She spent much of the next day with her infant son in her bedroom, avoiding contact with her mother.

By day four, the relational tension hit a boiling point when little Andy started crying because he couldn't get his model plane to fly.

Wanda: Amy, if your children ever received any discipline, they would be less likely to melt down like this.

Amy: Mom! I'm sick of listening to you describe my deficiencies as a parent. And while I'm at it, I don't want any more comments about my housekeeping, either!

Wanda: Well, I am sorry to disappoint you, dear, but I really can't be comfortable in a house with windows and floors in this condition.

Amy: I've had it! All you ever do is criticize me! Sure, you got an A+ for keeping your house clean when I was little, but that came at a cost, didn't it?! If you can't say something nice, then, please, say nothing.

Wanda: So *I'm* the problem here?! I didn't make your house a pigpen. I modeled a very different way of managing the house when you were little. If you weren't so focused on your career and hadn't moved clear across the country, your house would be clean, and we'd all get along!

Amy: Look, if you don't like the condition of my house or how I parent my children, there are some very nice hotels nearby! Stay there!

With this exchange, all the unspoken hurts came pouring out. This was new territory. Amy had never crossed her mom before. An icy tension filled the room, just as Amy's husband and father entered. The room stayed eerily silent for a minute or so, and then all parties went their separate ways. Amy took the baby to her bedroom to nurse, Dave suddenly remembered some important work he needed to do in the garage, and Howard went to the kitchen, where he poured himself a tall scotch. Soon after, Wanda and Howard cut their visit short and headed back to Ohio. Everyone was disappointed, and they each tell a different story of how they were victimized during the visit.

Let's look at this exchange through the lens of the A/P spectrum:

ACCEPTING/PROTECTING (A/P) SPECTRUM

ACCEPT				PROTECT
Destructively Over-Accepting Under-Protecting	Over-Accepting Under-Protecting	**IDEAL BALANCE**	Over-Protecting Under-Accepting	Destructively Over-Protecting Under-Accepting
PLEASERS →			← DEFENDERS	
Exploited Checked out Codependent Resentful Weak	Complacent People pleasing Capitulating Martyr Passive	Clear Reasonable Kind Courageous Satisfied	Controlling Intolerant Smug Critical Rigid	Aggressive Punitive Contentious Abandoning Manipulating
SELF-DESTRUCTIVE	SELF-DEPRIVING	SELF-RESPECTING	SELF-RIGHTEOUS	SELF-CENTERED

Wanda's passive-aggressive critiques land her squarely on the right-hand side of the A/P spectrum; she is controlling and critical. She shows signs of over-protecting in her self-righteous, self-absorbed responses and her "honest assessment" of Amy's housekeeping.

Amy initially responded to Wanda with her lifelong pattern of over-accepting: complacency, capitulation, and passivity. Then ultimately, she hit a wall and jumped from over-accepting to over-protecting; she became aggressive, contentious, and abandoning.

When we experience relational disappointment, it takes a lot of self-discipline to remember that we have a choice in how we respond. Will we respond in a constructive way or a destructive way? When we get hurt, scared, or angry, our primitive emotional brain takes over, and our fight-or-flight response kicks in. The problem with primitive, protective reactions is that they are designed to bring quick relief from "danger," which often comes at the expense of the relationship. When we're in the heat of battle, it takes a rugged commitment not to respond destructively to those who are disappointing or hurting us. In our triggered state, we actually believe that we'll feel better and safer if we choose a destructive response. We fool ourselves into feeling we're more in control.

We're easily tempted to succumb to these fight-or-flight reactions because, when we feel wronged, we're quick to believe we deserve a "pass" on the whole bridge-building business and are released to react in a retaliatory manner. In these heated moments, we give ourselves permission to lash out or to withdraw because we feel we're "just defending ourselves." And defending ourselves is a reasonable thing, right?

Destructive responses don't protect us. When the dust settles and our ability to think rationally reengages, we discover we were fooled again by our skittish brains, and now we've made the situation worse. Resorting to a destructive response when disappointed always results in a wider gap in the relationship. *Always.*

AVOID THE FOUR A'S OF MAKING THINGS WORSE

There are many ways we respond unproductively to our disappointments in the heat of battle, and I'd like to highlight four styles that most of us turn to:

1. *Aggression:* we get too big and controlling
2. *Avoidance:* we get too small and passive
3. *Abandonment:* we run away and withdraw
4. *Anesthesia:* we numb out and ignore

All four of these styles are destructive. They always make matters worse. We may resort to one style more frequently than others, but often we become experts at more than one style, depending on the situation. I may be prone to get aggressive when disappointed by my kids, anesthetize when disappointed by my spouse, get small and avoidant when disappointed by my boss, and withdraw into abandonment when disappointed by a friend. My guess is that there are times when you, like me, resort to each style as well.

RESORTING TO A DESTRUCTIVE RESPONSE WHEN DISAPPOINTED ALWAYS RESULTS IN A WIDER GAP IN THE RELATIONSHIP. *ALWAYS.*

None of us escapes the temptation to react to our disappointment in one of these destructive ways. It's human nature to try to defend ourselves when hurt. In addition, certain patterns of destructive responses were ingrained in us by our families of origin, and the examples modeled for us when we were kids. But we're not bound by those habits, patterns, or temptations. Once we're aware of our tendencies to respond destructively, we can catch ourselves in the moment and choose more productive, helpful responses. The key is awareness.

As we explore each of the destructive strategies in more detail, be attentive to the one(s) you're most likely to deploy. It's easier to catch yourself resorting to a destructive pattern when you know your blind spots.

1. Aggression

Aggression is a destructive style of responding to others that is characterized by the overuse or misapplication of power, or at least the appearance of power. When we resort to aggression, we attempt to get big by closing the gap through control, intimidation, or force. When we get aggressive, we're prone to respond to disappointment by over-protecting, and we try to create and maintain power-lopsided relationships. The characteristics on the right-hand side of the A/P spectrum are typically experienced by those around us who often interpret our conduct as self-righteous or self-absorbed.

Aggressive responses are not always physically threatening. They often start out more subtly, as we saw with Amy's mom. On the surface, Wanda seemed merely pushy and opinionated, but over time, her behavior became more destructive. This is common with the destructive strategy of aggression. Sometimes the aggression is direct and active ("If your children ever received any discipline . . ."), and sometimes it's passive ("Where's the Windex?").

Aggressive responses to disappointment typically escalate from passive-aggressive to controlling and, if left unchecked, to emotionally, spiritually, physically, or sexually abusive.

Physical Abuse

Abuse is a loaded word. So loaded, in fact, that I have never met an abusive person who did not resist or deny the suggestion that they exhibit any abusive behavior. Even people guilty of significant domestic violence somehow rationalize their behavior and deny that they're abusive. Most abusers begin by exerting themselves in such subtle ways that the word *abuse* doesn't fit. But abuse comes in many shapes and sizes. Some forms of abuse are explicitly horrible and easy to identify, including all acts of sexual and physical abuse. These acts of abuse require prompt and definitive action. While it's beyond the scope of this book to go into depth on physical or sexual abuse, allow me to share these three important points:

1. If you're the victim of any physical or sexual abuse, don't wait for things to get better on their own. They almost never do; in fact, they almost always become worse. Get help today. Contact the National Domestic Violence Hotline for next steps: 1–800-799-7233 (https://www.thehotline.org).

2. If you're the one causing or threatening to cause physical or sexual harm to someone in your home, or if people in your home fear you, I ask you to pack a bag right now and spend the night at a hotel or with a friend. Stay there until you get the help you need to stop abusing or threatening your loved ones. The people in your home deserve to fall asleep at night, every night, without fear of harm.

3. If you don't physically harm people in your home but make them emotionally or relationally afraid of you, this is still abuse. Seek help now. Again, your loved ones deserve to live in a fear-free environment.

Whether you're the abuser or the abused, physical abuse and intimidation must be stopped. Too many victims of such abuse wait too long to resist and become a tragic statistic. Don't become a statistic. Get help now.

Emotional and Verbal Abuse

More commonly, aggressive people often mishandle disappointment by using forms of abuse that are subtle and gradual in their corrosion: emotional and verbal abuse. Because this type of abuse is easier to justify than others, the abuser rarely considers their behavior to be abusive. But even subtle verbal and emotional jabs, over time, can kill a relationship. Think of it as death by 10,000 paper cuts.

Consider the case of Terri and Greg. Terri, one of the most successful sales representatives in her company, was promoted to regional manager of her territory. Greg has been a sales representative of the same company in a different branch for nearly ten years. They were peers until Terri's promotion. But with Terri in the role of boss, Greg began harboring some resentment, and Terri was feeling insecure about her new authority. Terri has a strong personality, and when disappointed, she resorts to the "A" of aggression. Their conversation might sound like this:

Terri: Greg, how did the Gateway people respond to today's new specs?

Greg: I'm meeting with them over breakfast tomorrow morning to present the specs and discuss.

Terri: Tomorrow? Didn't I ask all the reps to get specs out to clients today?!

Greg: Gateway's people prefer face-to-face, so I thought it would be better to meet with them in person.

Terri: We're not paying you "to think." I gave you reps clear instructions to send the specs out today. Let me tell you exactly what you're going to do. You're going to call Gateway, apologize for delaying their specs, and let them know that a new sales rep will call them before the end of the day.

Greg: What?! But they hate phone negotiations. And I've been their sales rep for almost ten years!

Terri: Sounds like nine and a half years too many, if you ask me.

Terri holds the upper hand in a power differential and (mis)uses her authority to inflict verbal abuse (insults) and emotional abuse (punitive decisions about his client list and a not-so-veiled threat about his job security), all in a misguided effort to resolve her own insecurity. She needs to remember that resorting to verbally or emotionally abusive tactics is always a destructive path and will eventually sour her leadership, influence, and relationships. Such over-protectors can't ignore an important life lesson when it comes to relationships: if we respond with aggression when facing disappointment, we "win the battle and lose the war."

2. Avoidance

When we resort to avoidance as our destructive response, we get small or disappear in the relationship and don't engage or deal with the situation. Avoidance is more common in a power-imbalanced relationship, in which we fear being rejected or harmed by the other person.

In avoidance, we tell ourselves the easiest way to manage this disappointment is to just live with it. Perhaps we justify our avoidant response with over-spiritualized statements such as, "I guess my [marriage/controlling mom/abusive boss] is just my cross to bear." Or, "I'm just trusting God to convict them about how they treat me. It's not my job to [judge/fix/correct] them."

Although it sounds benign, avoidance can actually cripple relationships. It always makes things worse. When we resort to avoidance, we surrender our God-given voice, autonomy, and agency. Avoidance not only damages the relationship between two people, it also damages our relationship with ourselves. It reinforces an internal lie that we're somehow less-than.

AVOIDANCE NOT ONLY DAMAGES THE RELATIONSHIP BETWEEN TWO PEOPLE, IT ALSO DAMAGES OUR RELATIONSHIP WITH OURSELVES.

Passive-aggressive responses are an offshoot of the avoidance pattern. In the workplace, a disappointed employee may use avoidance by becoming intentionally unavailable or unproductive. At home, a disappointed spouse may use avoidance by becoming silent.

Avoidance is one of my go-to habits. My wife will tell you that I can be famous for pouting and failing to engage in a mature conversation when I feel hurt. She tells me I've improved greatly over the years, but our conversations once sounded like this:

Me: [sulking in silence]

September: Are you okay? Is something wrong?

Me: Oh . . . I'm fine . . .

September: You don't sound fine.

Me: Well . . . it's nothing, really . . . I'll be fine . . .

Then I would pout until she cracked the code and figured out my problem or I felt pursued enough to reenter the conversation. Naturally, September would grow weary of this strategy and, out of frustration, would stop her pursuit and allow the gap to widen until I engaged more like a grown-up. In the end, I learned that using the avoidance strategy accomplished nothing more than muddying up the real issue and widening the gap for both of us.

In the case of Amy and her Windex-wielding mom, Wanda, Amy had learned decades ago that it was less stressful to give in to her mother's wishes. She learned that if she did not capitulate, Wanda would do little things to withhold her approval, which felt like withholding love, a significant threat for any child. Amy developed the pattern of getting small: not making waves, surrendering her legitimate desires, and silencing her voice whenever conflict arose.

In employing the avoidance strategy, we make a malignant trade.

We gain some short-term relief by resolving the tension with the other person. But it's a counterfeit relief, because it leads to resentment. Resentment starts as a small seed, but with every subsequent episode of capitulation and avoidance, it grows, and can lead to increasingly destructive forms of coping. As in Amy's case, the resentment grew until she exploded. People like Amy who feel oppressed often give themselves permission to rebel and defend themselves, which would be reasonable if they chose productive and protective strategies. But often they let the resentment build until the dam breaks, and then they flip from avoidance to aggression, causing further harm to the relationship and to themselves.

Amy's husband, Dave, chose another form of avoidance when the conflict arose: he said nothing and then slinked into his office. If he regularly retreats when things are hard, he'd be exhibiting the next form of destructive response: abandonment.

3. Abandonment

Abandonment is a form of avoidance that takes place when we desert the situation or relationship without first dealing with the issue and giving voice to what we're feeling, fearing, and desiring. It can be physical, when the person actually leaves, as Dave did with Amy, or emotional, when the person shuts down or stonewalls.

Isn't walking away from a relationship just one way of protecting ourselves? It's tricky. Many people guilty of abandonment will tell you that they're "just setting a boundary." But in my experience, people who choose abandonment as a way of coping with a difficult relational situation often haven't done an adequate job of right-sizing their disappointment or haven't taken ownership for their contributions to the gap. They simply hit a wall and walked away, creating greater distance, either physically or emotionally.

Remember, setting boundaries is a defensive move, not an offensive one. A true boundary is designed to keep the adverse effects of someone's bad behavior in their lap, not ours. With abandonment, we're often harboring resentment toward the other person and using physical or emotional distance as a weapon to hurt or control them.

We'll explore in part III that some situations require healthy protecting, in which we create significant space between us and the other person. In those cases, our process is a defensive move characterized by courage, wisdom, and humility. And our decision to create space is a strategy that maximizes our dignity, safety, and the chances of a healthy, albeit more distant, relationship with the other person. Abandonment, however, leaves both us and the other person worse off.

One variant of emotional abandonment occurs when, in our desire to escape the pain of the gap, we distract or numb ourselves, unintentionally abandoning the other person. This strategy can be referred to as anesthesia.

4. Anesthesia

Another way we sometimes mismanage the ache of our relational disappointments is to try to dull our discomfort. We use alcohol, drugs, pornography, video games, food, shopping, or any number of distractions to anesthetize ourselves. We may use more socially acceptable forms of numbing, such as overworking; becoming obsessed with exercise and health; going golfing or fishing; spending time on Facebook or becoming consumed with other addicting hobbies; or becoming overly involved with church, volunteering, or parenting our children.

Some of the things we use to anesthetize ourselves aren't harmful in appropriate doses. The problem occurs when we abuse these things for the purpose of numbing our pain. Anesthetizing fails to lessen our relational disappointments; it does not get to the root issue and causes new problems. In fact, the disappointment not only waits for us, it often grows like a cancer while we're distracted. Those who anesthetize often have subconscious resentment against others and themselves, making the relational problem worse, often in powerfully destructive ways.

In the story of Amy and Wanda, anesthetizing played a factor. When things got tense in the home, Amy's father, Howard, immediately headed for the kitchen and poured himself a drink. My guess is that this has been his coping mechanism for many years, leaving Amy feeling abandoned as a child, and slowly contributing to the disintegration of his marriage. Behind Howard's drinking is an avoidance problem. He doesn't have the courage to find his voice, confront his wife about her controlling ways, and advocate for himself or his daughter, so he resorts to drinking.

When we explore our own tendency toward anesthetizing our pain, we must navigate the fine line between anesthetizing, which is a distracting, destructive counterfeit, and self-soothing, which is a healthy way to calm ourselves in the face of disappointment so we can respond in humble and productive ways. The continuum looks like this:

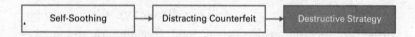

The difference between choosing a healthy, self-soothing activity and resorting to a counterfeit often shows itself in our motives. We choose self-soothing activities to help us refuel, get centered, or gain perspective *so that* we can reengage our relational disappointment in a healthy way. When we choose distracting or destructive counterfeits to avoid pain, we do so to avoid responding to our disappointment, often at the expense of the relationship. We might choose to play our favorite video game for ten minutes to calm down after a heated conversation, so we can then reengage in the conversation in a healthier way (self-soothing); or we might choose to numb ourselves by holing up in the basement, playing the same video game hours on end, as a way to avoid the heated conversation altogether (distracting or destructive counterfeit). Same activity; different motives.

There is no upside to using one of these four A's—aggression, avoidance, abandonment, and anesthesia—when reacting to relational disappointments. These responses always cause destruction in our relationships and in ourselves. Yet we're still tempted to reach for one of them when our pain gets triggered. How can we make better choices in the heat of battle? This is a critical question, because there are tremendous upsides to resisting behaviors that widen the gap. And no matter how your troubled relationship turns out, you'll have the peace of mind that comes from looking back on your own conduct with deep satisfaction. The goal is no regrets.

> WE CHOOSE SELF-SOOTHING ACTIVITIES TO HELP US REFUEL, GET CENTERED, OR GAIN PERSPECTIVE *SO THAT* WE CAN REENGAGE OUR RELATIONAL DISAPPOINTMENT IN A HEALTHY WAY.

A Story from the Home Front: My Pattern of Making Things Worse

Both in my own life and in those with whom I interact, I've noticed a pattern: we're most tempted to react destructively when the situation pokes a core fear in our lives. We all have core fears, such as fears of betrayal, abandonment, exploitation, loss of safety and security, and the like. These are a natural development of childhood, and, depending on our unique childhood and adult experiences, they sometimes linger on, wreaking havoc in our relationships.

The core fears I brought from childhood into adulthood relate to being abandoned, dismissed, or discarded. This fear translates into an irrational fear, a paranoia at times, when relationships get tense. The lie I carried into adulthood was, *People can't be trusted.* Or, when I encounter relational discord, *The other person wants to dismiss or reject me.*

This core fear tempts me to interpret the other person's disappointment in me as both personal and dangerous. My hypervigilance leaves me feeling unnecessarily threatened, and I exaggerate the gap. And when I get triggered, I'm prone to reach for one of the destructive defensive strategies. My favorites are aggression and avoidance, though I'm pretty proficient at all four. As you might have guessed, I'm most likely to resort to a destructive response with the people I'm closest to. Nowhere have I blown it more than in my marriage.

September's core fear from childhood is not being important or valued. She was the oldest of two children, and her younger brother, Greg, was born with cerebral palsy and an intellectual disability. Particularly in his early years, Greg had substantial medical and developmental problems that required much focus and time from her parents. September interpreted that it was her job in the family not to be a burden, not to have needs that would distract her parents from her brother, and to ease their burden by being the perfect child. Of course, this was not the message her parents intended to send. But, as is so often true for us as kids, we do our best to make sense of our circumstances. As a result, September entered adulthood believing the lie, *My needs don't matter as much as other people's needs. I'm only lovable when I'm perfect.*

September's core fears and mine collided when we married. My fear of being abandoned or betrayed left me hypervigilant about her flaws; and her fear of being unloved or devalued if she was imperfect left her defensive and resistant to even the slightest negative feedback. I managed my fear with critique and control (aggression), while she managed her fear with defensiveness and deceit (a variation of avoidance and abandonment). In other words, I made our gap worse by responding with aggression; September made our gap worse by responding with avoidance and abandonment.

It was the perfect storm. The more I criticized her and responded with aggression, the more September responded with resistance, avoidance, and abandonment. The more she avoided and abandoned, the more my fears were provoked, and I responded with increased critique and aggression. Each of us chose destructive responses to our own core fears that turned out to be gasoline on the other's core-fear fire.

It took years of this destructive, crazy cycle before we were able to recognize our patterns and make the necessary efforts to address our own contributions to the gap. Sadly, we hurt each other considerably and allowed our marriage to teeter perilously close to a terminal cliff before we figured this out and chose a new path—one of healing, forgiveness, and learning how to respond in healthier ways when our fears got triggered.

Today September and I have the marriage we had always dreamed about. She calls it "the sweetest marriage of all the marriages!" which always makes me grin, given our bumpy road to get here. That painful era feels like ancient history now, but we stay mindful of our past because we don't want to slip back into our toxic ways. We both agree that learning not to make things worse with destructive responses—partnered with the concepts you'll read about in the next two chapters of this book—saved our marriage, and matured it into the mutually fulfilling relationship it is today.

GRABBING THE REINS OF YOUR FEARS

If you screwed up your relationships as often as I have, eventually you'll notice patterns in your behavior. Recognizing these patterns when you're disappointed and triggered helps protect you from making things worse.

One such pattern is this: when our core fears get triggered and we feel we're at relational risk, we tend to start listening to internal voices of distorted self-talk, such as:

- *People aren't safe. It's better to withdraw.*
- *He's going to reject me.*
- *There's something wrong with me that makes people abandon me.*

- *She's going to hurt me, so I'd better protect myself.*
- *If I resist, I'll get fired.*
- *She won't like me if I stand up for myself.*

These distortions feed our fears. They're not rational, but they *feel* rational when we're triggered. When we know we're prone to this kind of self-talk, we can push pause and ask ourselves how we're distorting reality. We can then counter those distorted voices by repeating certain phrases that remind us of what's true, such as:

- "It's okay to be disappointed, but it's not okay to make things worse."
- "Disappointment is normal. I don't have to make a big deal every time it comes around."
- "What are the facts? What should this person's past affection, friendship, and loyalty teach me about this present situation?"
- "Just because the other person is disappointed doesn't mean I'm being rejected."

I am shocked at how often these little phrases and questions calm, redirect, and protect me from making things worse. I may still feel sad, angry, or disappointed. But this little self-soothing practice helps me to step out of the paranoid, triggered state that so often sabotages my relationships, and instead to choose helpful responses that right-size the gap. Translation: I don't make things worse.

When your core fears get triggered and you're tempted to make things worse by choosing a destructive response, what phrases can you choose to help you step back into a rational, calm, and realistic state? Come up with a handful of your own easy-to-remember phrases like those above, and then commit them to memory so they'll be waiting for you when you need them. This simple step can help you keep from making matters worse.

Once we have minimized the risk of making things worse, we can dive into the most critical step of discerning how to proceed in difficult relationships: right-sizing the gap.

SIX

What Do I *Really* Want?

WHERE WE'RE HEADED:

- Gain clarity on your gap by getting clear on your desires

The costliest mistake most of us make when managing our disappointment is to take action before we have a clear understanding of the gap. To see the full scope of our disappointment by right-sizing the gap, let's begin by defining each part of the "problem of life" model:

- *Reality:* how you perceive the relationship today
- *Desire:* what you want for the relationship in the future
- *The Gap:* the distance between today's reality and your desires for the future—your disappointment

Right-Size the Gap

Getting an accurate, undistorted assessment of our gaps is harder than it seems. Most of us tend to distort our gaps in one of two ways: by thinking and behaving as if the gap is *bigger* than it really is, or by thinking and behaving as if the gap is *smaller* than it really is. In either case, a misunderstood gap leaves us likely to choose a less-than-ideal balance of accepting and protecting. We'll overreact or underreact, sabotaging our goal of relational peace, harmony, and satisfaction.

Accuracy matters when it comes to right-sizing the gap. Getting off course early, even by a tiny amount, will greatly limit the likelihood of reaching our relational destinations. Even a small margin of error is costly. It pays, therefore, to invest time in understanding our gaps, so we can then right-size those gaps with precision and accuracy.

DIAGNOSIS: THE IMPORTANCE OF ACCURATELY ASSESSING OUR GAPS

Before becoming a pastor in 2002, I was a practicing physician. On the surface, this looks like a significant career shift. But I have been pleasantly surprised by the overlap in my two seemingly different careers. They both involve helping people in crisis or pain, and they both require that I take steps to make an accurate "diagnosis" of someone's situation before offering a helpful course of treatment. In many ways, my first career as an attending physician in the emergency department did a better job at preparing me to be a pastor than did my seminary degree.

One of the most important medical imperatives for a physician is to accurately diagnose the root cause of a patient's symptoms before initiating a treatment plan. We have all heard stories of a patient who was overtreated, undertreated, or mistreated because of an inaccurate diagnosis. Many of the avoidable catastrophic medical outcomes I witnessed in the emergency department were often due to inadequate attention to this vital first step during a patient's earlier visit to a doctor's office or urgent-care clinic. In these cases, the physician likely failed to invest the proper time, care, or knowledge in the diagnosis stage before applying a treatment strategy.

The more critically ill a patient presents upon arrival, the more careful and methodical physicians must be in accurately diagnosing what's really going on. In medicine, we must get the correct diagnosis before prescribing treatment. So it is in managing our relational disappointments. If we "treat" a gap before carefully and accurately diagnosing it, we risk causing relational malpractice and widening the gap.

I can guess what you might be thinking:

- *But I've been dealing with this person for years.*
- *I already understand the problem. I don't need to spend any more time thinking about it.*
- *I just want to do something!*

And to that, I would ask you—maybe even beg you—to keep reading.

The vast majority of us, even when we're in chronically disappointing relational situations, fail to take the necessary, focused time to truly clarify and right-size the gap. By neglecting to invest the time, we may apply the right solutions to the wrong problems, and perhaps have been doing so for years, or even decades.

> IF WE "TREAT" A GAP BEFORE CAREFULLY AND ACCURATELY DIAGNOSING IT, WE RISK CAUSING RELATIONAL MALPRACTICE AND WIDENING THE GAP.

Commit to investing the time necessary to get true clarity on your situation. In doing so, you'll get better results by applying the right solutions in the relationship. Trust me, you won't regret this investment of your time.

Two Questions That Bring Clarity to Your Gaps

A relational gap is the span between our desired outcome in a relationship and our perceived reality. We right-size our gaps by getting clarity on the characteristics of these borders that define them.

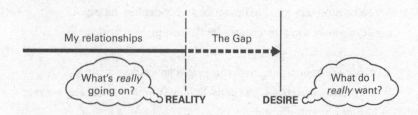

We do this by asking two crucial questions: The first question, What do I *really* want? helps clarify our desired outcome for a relationship. The second question, What's *really* going on? helps us better understand a relationship's current reality. We'll tackle the first question in this chapter and the second question in the next chapter.

Answering the question, What do I *really* want? with accuracy requires an injection of both time and humility. If you're like me, your first pass at answering this question might be a bit self-serving. Let me share two examples, one from my own life and one from a married couple who asked to meet with me.

A Story from the Home Front:
Recurring Conflict over Punctuality

The Vaudrey punctuality versus flexibility conflict is something my wife and I struggled with for years, as I mentioned earlier. It took a painful toll on us relationally. Things changed for me one spring morning when September was supposed to meet me at Starbucks after I dropped off my car to get its studded winter tires replaced with all-season tires for spring. I checked my car in, walked across the parking lot to Starbucks, and arrived on time—that is, five minutes early.

September was not there. *Shock!*

I got my coffee, found a table, and immediately began my favorite ritual: internally whining, seething, and feeling sorry for myself because my wife was once again late. But this time I felt a twinge of conviction: *Hmmm. I'm blaming this whole pattern on my wife. Maybe I should assess my role in this punctuality dance.* Granted, being habitually late was not September's finest quality. But I knew in my gut that I was contributing to the resulting unhealthy process too. What exactly was my contribution?

At that time, I had just read a fantastic new book, *Crucial Conversations*.[1] Sitting there with my coffee, one particular section of the book flooded back to my mind. It proposed five questions to ask ourselves before any difficult conversation. I thought, *What were those questions?*

I fired up my laptop, opened my highlights from the book (yes, I save and catalog my highlights from books; I'm nerdy that way), and found the five questions. I knew I had a good fifteen minutes to get honest with myself before September arrived, so I opened up my journal and started a new entry.

The book's first question was, What do I *really* want? Easy. I typed my first gut response: "I want a wife who's a responsible adult!"

I read what I'd written. *Hmm. Maybe a little harsh, and rather self-righteous.* This often happens when I first tackle this question. My early responses are distorted to bolster my position, rather than to help me look deeper and gain a more accurate assessment of my desires for the relationship. If you struggle with first responses, too, don't be discouraged. Our initial responses are important, because they get us thinking. The more honest, vulnerable, and helpful answers to the question will reveal themselves if we keep digging.

I kept typing: "Why does September's lateness bother me so much?"

It's terrifying for me to admit that I have a personal need. I'm not proud of this, but it's true. When a personal need goes unmet in my marriage, I'm much more comfortable making it about September's flaw rather than about my need. This arrangement allows me to stay righteously indignant, and my early responses often reflect this. Such was the case in that Starbucks.

But as I sat there thinking, I had to admit my righteous indignity was getting me nowhere. My wife continued being late, and I kept getting more worked up about it than seemed reasonable. I knew, down deep, that this issue was about more than mere punctuality.

As you engage this process for yourself, be patient on your response to this first question. Take plenty of time to write and reflect on your answers, because your initial gut response almost always misses the point. At least it does with me. If I had stopped journaling after my initial snotty answer to the first question, I would have done little more than justify my indignation and reinforce my one-sided point of view. Then, when September arrived, I would have greeted her with yet another hurtful and unproductive response, perpetuating my contribution to our unhealthy pattern.

I reread my first response: "I want a wife who is a responsible adult!" *Sigh. That's not it.* Clearly, my wife, who masterfully manages our home, her own writing projects, and the care and nurturing of our five kids, was generally a responsible adult.

I kept writing: "I want my time to be honored."

Sounds closer. And what makes this statement harder to evaluate is that it happens to be true. At some level, lateness *is* dishonoring to the person left waiting. So it would have been easy for me to stop my self-reflections there. When September arrived, I could have felt justified in protesting, "I am sick and tired of my time being wasted!" But then I would have missed getting what I really wanted.

While there may be tiny slivers of truth in our early responses, those responses are often our attempts to justify our self-serving reactions. Deep down I knew that my time being dishonored was not the root issue. In fact, on that particular morning my time wasn't even being wasted. I could easily have been filling those minutes working on a project on my laptop. September wasn't holding me back. But still, there I sat, paralyzed by anger. The only one dishonoring my time was me.

I asked myself again, "Why does this bother me so much?" I

tried to stop pouting and really sit with what I was feeling. I kept digging for a more honest and complete answer to that first question. And eventually I came to an important realization: *I'm not angry. I'm hurt . . . and afraid.*

I kept journaling. This time I wrote: "I want to feel valued by my wife. I want to know I'm important to her. When she's late, I feel unimportant. When she makes me wait, I feel devalued."

Ouch. That was hard to admit. But I knew right away I had reached a more honest answer. Whenever September was late, even if it was for a legitimate reason, I took it personally. I felt devalued or unimportant. I took it as a sign that she didn't really care about me. And yet, for years, I'd truly believed the issue was punctuality.

The paradox was striking: the emotions I was *actually* feeling inside were fear and hurt, yet the emotion I expressed to September was anger.

What do I *really* want? "I want reassurance of my wife's love."

I then continued on to the rest of the five questions. Here's an excerpt from my journal that day:

- *Question Two:* How would I behave if I really did want this?
  Oh dear. If I want reassurance of my wife's love, I would behave *the opposite* of how I am behaving right now.
- *Question Three:* What do I not want?
  I don't want more distance from September. I don't want her to resent me because I respond so angrily every time she's late.
- *Question Four:* What am I acting like I really want?
  Like I want *more* distance from my wife, not less. Like I want to give her a good reason to put distance between us. I'm pretty much acting the *exact opposite* of how I should be acting. Oh boy. I need to change my strategy.
- *Question Five:* How should I go about getting what I really want and avoid getting what I don't want?

Wow. By changing my approach, maybe I could actually get what I really want (a reassurance of September's love), rather than what I've been demanding all these years (a wife who isn't late).

This process was very helpful. If I had stopped digging deeper after my early, self-justifying responses, I would have continued thinking my core desire was to have a wife who honors my time by being prompt. I'd still be confronting September about her tardiness and nagging her about her disrespecting my precious time, and she would still be reacting defensively, feeling micromanaged and demeaned. She might have become more punctual simply to avoid dealing with my anger, not because she values me. I would have gotten what I *thought* I wanted (September showing up on time) at the expense of what I *really* wanted (feeling valued and closer to my wife). By failing to accurately diagnose my desires all these years, I had widened the gap and then applied unproductive responses: anger and control.

When September finally arrived at the coffee shop that morning (eleven minutes late, not that I noticed), she apologized for making me wait. I was able to control my response to her lateness and, armed with new insight, I owned my contributions to this ongoing dance. We then engaged in the first of several honest, productive conversations about an issue that had plagued our relationship for years.

As an ironic aside, once I stopped being my wife's punctuality sheriff, she became curious as to why she seemed unable to master this one area of her life. She did her own inner digging, asking herself those five helpful questions. And once she became internally motivated to grow in this area, her punctuality greatly improved. It turned out, when I got clear on what I really wanted and stopped trying to control my wife, she did a better job of controlling herself. Who knew?

Today, September is usually punctual, though she still has a more relaxed relationship with time—and probably always will—than I do, which is a nice counterbalance to my intensity. We've learned to navigate this gap without hurting each other.

Developing the habit of asking, What do I *really* want? will help you better understand the desires side of the gap equation and, as a result, greatly improve your relationships with coworkers, friends, and family. When you're disappointed with a relational situation, ask yourself that crucial first question before reacting. And do some honest digging until you gain the insight you need. Otherwise you're likely to mislabel your true desires, react poorly, and widen the gap. You'll get what you ask for, at the expense of what you really want.

A Story of Will and Mary

I first met with Mary when she and Will had been married for eighteen years. She described Will as unhappy, unmotivated, and unemployed. "The first several years of our marriage were great," she said. "But problems bubbled up around year seven, after our third kid was born."

With three preschoolers at home, they both agreed Mary would quit her job and stay home full time. Will made good money as a construction worker, so they tightened their budget and lived off his income. But then Will injured his back playing football with friends—and it cost him his job. Eventually his back injury required surgery, which went well. During months of rehabilitation, he remained unable to

DEVELOPING THE HABIT OF ASKING, WHAT DO I *REALLY* WANT? WILL HELP YOU BETTER UNDERSTAND THE DESIRES SIDE OF THE GAP EQUATION AND, AS A RESULT, GREATLY IMPROVE YOUR RELATIONSHIPS WITH COWORKERS, FRIENDS, AND FAMILY.

work so he collected unemployment. But then the unemployment checks ran out, and Mary had to go back to work, leaving Will to care for their kids at home.

"But despite being all healed up from his back surgery, he does the bare minimum with the kids, and does even less to help around the house." Mary said. "It's been two years since his surgery, and he's still unemployed. He won't even look for a job! I was very patient at first. But he's healed up now, and it's been two years! My job doesn't pay that well, and we've spent most of our savings just to pay the bills. I'm now the sole provider financially, and when I come home from work, the house is trashed, laundry's overflowing, and the kids are hungry and bored. What does Will do all day? No matter how many lists I leave for him or how many times I ask for more help, nothing changes. Now, when I walk in the door and see the house like that, I either seethe inside or just lose it!"

Mary's level of anger was understandable, considering how absent her husband had been. She felt hopeless, and now wanted out of the marriage. Will's behavior since losing his job had created a sizable gap in their relationship. But was Will's behavior the sole cause of the gap or was there more? And was Mary's strategy of list making, nagging, and endlessly venting her frustration narrowing the gap with Will or widening it? What does Mary *really* want?

After listening to the full brunt of Mary's frustrations, I asked that very question. Here's how our conversation went:

Mary: What do I really want? That's easy. I *really* want a *real* husband. I want someone who contributes. I want Will to get off his butt and get a job!

Me: Makes sense. I agree that for Will to succeed in his relationship with you and the kids, he needs to contribute more at home and financially. I wonder, though, if there is more to your dream relationship with Will than finances and practical help. What would your ideal marriage with him look like?

Mary: Are you kidding?! We're so far from that, I can't even imagine.

Mary's first response sounded a lot like my early response to my wife's punctuality. I tried to help Mary dig a little deeper.

Me: I'm not asking you to dream up the *perfect* marriage. But imagine that Will suddenly found a good job and started making decent money. Would that be the happy ending you're looking for? What would be different?

Mary: Well, for one thing, we could pay our bills!

Me: Great. Would that solve everything?

Mary: Well, it would sure help. But no, that wouldn't solve everything. It's not just about the money. He needs to pull his own weight around the house too. And help more with the kids. He just lets them sit in front of the TV all day. He contributes the absolute bare minimum.

It was obvious Mary felt deeply wounded by Will's lack of contributions in a number of areas. Her frustrations made sense. And she recognized it wasn't just about the money, but about his lack of being a good partner. She was getting closer to the root issue.

Me: For the sake of argument, imagine that Will becomes a household machine and does all the upkeep of the house and yard while you're at work, and becomes Super Dad to your kids. Would your marital disappointment be solved? Would you be happy then?

Mary grew quiet, and her eyes filled. She sat silently for a minute before continuing.

> **Mary:** Well, it would be a great improvement. But to be honest, that would not solve all of it. For these past two years, I have just felt so alone. Ever since Will's back injury, he's turned inward. He shows me no affection, no tenderness, no attention. My husband and I used to be the best partners. But we don't communicate anymore. We used to be teammates. Now we're on opposing teams. I hate it. I'm just so lonely.

By working through her early responses to the question, What do I *really* want? Mary recognized that Will's unemployment and lack of help with the kids and home were significant wounds, but they were not the root issue.

What did Mary really want? "I just want my husband back," Mary said. "I want him to be my loving life partner and teammate again. We were so good at that. We were a team. It was always us against the world. Now it's just us against us."

Mary had been emotionally abandoned by Will during their challenging circumstances. And she'd contributed to their problems by how she responded to him. She now had clarity on the root issue: the fracture in their "us against the world" partnership. She still loved Will. She valued him as her life partner and wanted him back.

But none of us has the power to change another person. If Will refuses to make progress in these areas, Mary will have some hard decisions to make. What should she do now? How should she respond? What can each of us do with our gaps when we're powerless to change the person who is disappointing us?

Although we cannot change other people, we are not powerless. We have full control over how we respond when they disappoint us. If Will continues to stay closed off and inattentive to Mary's needs—financially, practically, and emotionally—she gets to choose how she'll respond. She is in control of whatever steps she chooses to take in her marriage. She's also in control of her capacity to not contribute to widening the gap.

Mary and Will still had much to learn about setting healthy boundaries. But in my office that day, I was impressed by how Mary had invested the necessary time and humility to answer the question, What do I *really* want? After working past her condescending first answers, she was able to get to the root issue of what she really wanted: a life partnership with the husband she loved. This reality doesn't negate or minimize the tangible problems that currently exist with Will's lack of contribution. But, clarity on her desires helps Mary to not fall into the trap of getting what she's asking for (a compliant husband) at the expense of what she *really* wants (a loving life partner).

> ALTHOUGH WE CANNOT CHANGE OTHER PEOPLE, WE ARE NOT POWERLESS. WE HAVE FULL CONTROL OVER HOW WE RESPOND WHEN THEY DISAPPOINT US.

With this clarity, Mary felt a tiny spark of hope for their future. She decided to put any divorce proceedings on hold while she reconfigured and right-sized her disappointment. Before we ended our conversation, she asked for a recommendation of a good counselor. I gave her referrals to three licensed therapists who could help her work through this complex situation. (We'll pick up Mary and Will's story in chapter 7.)

Getting clarity on the "desires" side of the gap helps us identify the deepest longings we have for our relationships. But asking, What do I *really* want? is only half of the story. The other half of right-sizing the gap is a more formidable challenge. The second border of the gap—What's *really* going on?—is where we're headed next.

SEVEN

REALITY: WHAT'S
Really GOING ON?

WHERE WE'RE HEADED:

- Get clear on reality: What's *really* going on?
- Understand the stretching style of self-deception
- Understand the shrinking style of self-deception

I need to begin this chapter with two disclaimers. First, the concepts in this chapter will poke at parts of you that make you uncomfortable. I don't apologize for this. The very parts of us that need the most honing are the ones that need poking. If you're motivated to do what it takes to improve troubled relationships, you can handle it. Second, this chapter is dreadfully long, and I do apologize for this. But rather than dividing this content into smaller chapters, I feel you're better served by looking at these concepts as one unit. Feel free to take a seventh-inning stretch at either (or both) of the section breaks: stretching self-deception or shrinking self-deception. Ready? Let's dive in.

We all have a tendency to tell ourselves, and totally believe, a distorted version of reality that makes us feel better about ourselves. In my punctuality example with my wife in the previous chapter, as I sat there fuming because September was late, I told myself, "She's *always* late and *I'm* never late!" Which, of course, wasn't true. However, by telling myself this distorted version of reality, I felt more justified in my anger.

We all do this. We distort reality to help us feel better about our responses to being hurt or disappointed. Those who tend to be protectors and over-protect will often exaggerate, making the gap seem bigger than it really is, as I did while waiting for my wife. Those who tend to be acceptors and over-accept will often minimize the gap, making it seem less troubling than it really is, so we can justify our underreactions. This inclination to distort reality in either direction is called self-deception, and it affects us all. It's human nature.

And it's catastrophic to relationships.

IDENTIFYING SELF-DECEPTION

Self-deception is a tendency to distort the truth so we feel better about our choices, our behaviors, and ourselves. To understand this naturally occurring phenomenon, let's engage in a quick exercise.

Exercise: Name and Describe Someone Who Is Remarkable

1. *On a sheet of paper, draw two columns:* Label the left column, "List 1: Remarkable people," and the right column, "List 2: Character traits."

LIST 1: REMARKABLE PEOPLE	LIST 2: CHARACTER TRAITS

2. *In List 1, write the names of several people you deeply respect and admire:* They can be public figures, historical figures, or people you know. We each know or have read about people who exhibit character traits we find particularly remarkable. They consistently respond to situations in ways that are right and good.

Here's my List 1, in no particular order:

LIST 1: REMARKABLE PEOPLE	LIST 2: CHARACTER TRAITS
Dr. Robert Bocksch Jim Pluymert Ruth Bader Ginsberg George Washington Mother Teresa Dan Allender	

My list includes my hero and mentor, Dr. Robert Bocksch, who was chairperson of the chemistry department at Whitworth College, where I was a biochemistry major back in the 1980s. Bocksch was a deeply respected professor who set high standards for his students, yet he went out of his way to be kind and attentive to me. I will always remember him for his intelligence, care, and discernment.

I included my friend Jim Pluymert for his gentleness and goodness, and Supreme Court Justice Ruth Bader Ginsberg for her powerful story of rising above the glass ceiling for women in the field of law. I'm a bit of a history geek, so I included George Washington for his selfless courage, integrity, and dedication to our nation. I listed Mother Teresa for her unconditional acceptance of others and her self-sacrifice. And I wrote down another hero and mentor, Dan Allender, whose discernment has helped, and continues to help, me gain clarity in my life.

3. *In List 2, write down the specific character traits you most admire about these people:* Name the attributes that make these people remarkable. What traits do they possess that make them stand out to you? Here are my List 2 character traits:

LIST 1: REMARKABLE PEOPLE	LIST 2: CHARACTER TRAITS
Dr. Robert Bocksch	kind, strong, brilliant
Jim Pluymert	gentle, good
Ruth Bader Ginsberg	self-confident, disciplined
George Washington	courageous, honest, honorable, dedicated
Mother Teresa	accepting of others, self-sacrificing
Dan Allender	discerning, bold

What traits did you write down? I suspect a few overlap with mine.

Okay, now it gets real. As you review your List 2 character traits, ask yourself the following questions:

- Does this list describe me?
- Are each of these traits true of me?
- Do I consistently live out all these traits?

If you answered yes to any of these questions, then you either have no need to read this book or have deeper relational problems than this book can solve. Hopefully, for your sake and the sake of your loved ones, your answer to each question was an honest, "No, I'm not remarkable in *all* these ways, *all* the time." Of course not. Neither am I, not by a long shot. No one consistently lives out all these positive attributes all the time. When I look at my List 2, I am saddened by the number of character traits I admire but cannot consistently claim as my own.

And here's an even more uncomfortable truth about me: I desperately want you, and everyone else I know, *to think* that I possess all these remarkable traits all the time. And therein lies the problem. We want others to believe we're better than we really are. It's human nature. And it's the seed of self-deception.

Every day, you and I are confronted with promptings to do something that is right and good—to behave in a manner that someone from List 1 would behave. Whether we believe these promptings come from God or from our own consciences, we all get these types of inner nudges. Maybe the prompting is something small: take a moment to encourage our waitress at the diner, hold the door open for someone at the store, or let a fellow driver merge into traffic ahead of us. Sometimes the prompting is more substantial: apologize for your part of an argument, politely stand up for someone when your boss is unkind to them, or tell your spouse the whole truth about your inappropriate relationship with that person, substance, or activity.

> WE WANT OTHERS TO BELIEVE WE'RE BETTER THAN WE REALLY ARE. IT'S HUMAN NATURE. AND IT'S THE SEED OF SELF-DECEPTION.

Whether small or substantial, we get these promptings to do something right and good every single day. We then have a chance to either behave like our List 1 people and follow through or to ignore the prompting. If the good thing we're prompted to do is something that comes easily—something we would do automatically—then we hardly notice the prompting and just obey it. But sometimes a prompting requires us to behave counter to our usual patterns or desires. If saying yes to these promptings requires more effort or sacrifice than we feel like making, the temptation to self-deceive raises its ugly head.

ANATOMY OF SELF-DECEPTION

In their fantastic book, *Leadership and Self-Deception*, the Arbinger Institute captures an insightful observation I want to build upon in this next section. Every time we receive promptings, we have an inner sense of how our List 1 people would respond. We face a choice: Will we obey the prompting or ignore it? (In Arbinger's language and graphic, Will we honor the feeling or betray it?[1])

Sometimes we obey, behaving like our List 1 people: we clean up the scrap of litter we see on the ground, hold the elevator door open for the guy running to catch it, or have the hard conversation with someone we care about. When we obey these promptings to do something right and good, we feel content inside. We feel *satisfied*.

For example, a few months back, I was driving to work. Traffic was heavy, and another lane was merging into mine. In my side mirror, I noticed someone trying to sneak up on the shoulder and pass a bunch of us decent, law-abiding citizens who were driving in a manner consistent with civilized society. This guy wanted to cut in front of me instead of waiting his turn. *The nerve!* When this happens, a juvenile part of me usually wants to play traffic-justice vigilante and block the offender out. It would've been quite easy for me to tailgate the guy ahead of me so the cheater couldn't possibly wedge his way in. I'm not proud of this tendency, but I don't like cheaters. (I confess that on some days, I give in to my temptation.)

But on this particular morning, I sensed a clear prompting: "Let the guy in." In other words, stop acting as if I know the motivation or circumstance causing this man to behave like a traffic barbarian. Don't be a jerk and block him out. Instead, just slow down and wave him in.

First, I complained about the prompting. *But he's cheating!*

Yet for whatever reason, counter to my usual leaning, I slowed down and waved the guy in. He pulled ahead of me and then waved with appreciation. And I thought, *Wow, I'm a swell guy.* I felt satisfied.

Here's how it works:

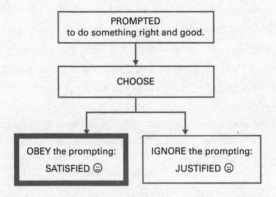

Granted, it was a small victory. When we behave in a manner consistent with the character traits we captured in List 2, we feel glad we did something right and good.

On the contrary, when we ignore a prompting to do something good and right, we feel a certain level of discomfort inside. Twangs of conviction create dissonance in us because we want to see ourselves as admirable, like the List 1 people who consistently display List 2 character traits. So when a prompting is difficult or inconvenient, we're tempted to relieve our discomfort by turning to self-deception. We tell ourselves a different story, one that is slightly distorted from reality. But the new story allows us to still feel good about ourselves even as we're actively choosing *not* to do something good. In those circumstances, we feel *justified*.

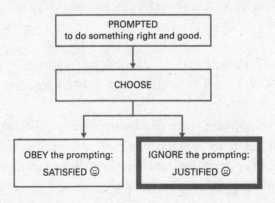

Crazy? Yes. But we do it all the time. I do this, and so do you. I can think of countless times when I received a prompting to do something right and good—something my List 1 people would automatically do—but chose to ignore it. I then immediately turned to self-deception by telling a new and distorted story, so I didn't feel like a jerk. Here are some of the stories I've told:

PROMPTINGS I'VE RECEIVED	MY SELF-JUSTIFYING STORIES
Buy the homeless man some food.	Better not. He'll just be disappointed that I didn't give him cash.
Hold the elevator door for the guy running toward me.	Nope. I don't want to make the others in the elevator wait.
Apologize to September.	No. She might use it against me later.
Help my coworker with the project he's running behind on.	No way. I don't want to enable his pattern of procrastination.

When we receive promptings we'd rather ignore, we're tempted to create a distortion of the story that helps relieve the dissonance we feel inside. We want to believe, and we want others to believe, that we're just like our List 1 people who do right and good things. But when our conduct suggests otherwise, we tell ourselves a distorted story, which leaves us feeling justified, rather than satisfied. We all justify ourselves in this manner, often subconsciously and instantaneously. This is self-deception.

Stretching and Shrinking: Two Styles of Self-Deception

We use two different styles of self-deception to create stories that justify our failure to do something right and good: stretching and shrinking. They're aptly named, based on the impact they have on the relational gap we're trying to manage.

Both styles originate from the same basic tension: we want to feel better about ourselves, our behaviors, and our decisions; and we want to soothe our discomfort from behaving in a manner inconsistent with the admirable character traits of our List 1 people. Both styles are destructive to relationships.

The stretching style of self-deception tries to make the gap seem bigger than it really is. The shrinking style of self-deception tries to make the gap appear smaller than it really is. While we all utilize both styles, depending on the circumstances, each of us tends to be more effective with one style over the other. It's important to understand each style so we can easily identify our own tendencies to distort reality.

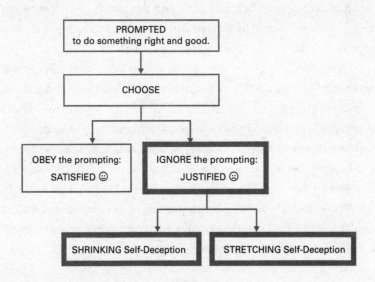

Stretching Self-Deception

When we use the stretching style of self-deception, we distort reality so that the gap seems bigger than it actually is, and we interpret the other person and their behaviors as *worse* than they really are, while making ourselves *better* than we really are. We can then justify our desire to shift into protection mode more quickly, even when the situation may actually call for accepting and building a bridge.

You've possibly guessed by now that my go-to style of justifying my bad choices would be *stretching self-deception*, and you'd be right. Here's a story from my marriage that demonstrates this style of self-deception.

A Story from the Home Front: September's Gas Tank

While our children were growing up, the kids and I had a Mother's Day ritual for my wife and her beloved vegetable garden. We would all pile into September's minivan and take her to as many nurseries as necessary to buy seeds, bedding flowers, and vegetable starts, which she would then plant, care for, and cultivate for the rest of the summer. Gardening gave her, and still gives her, much joy. All summer long, our family would be blessed with the most delicious—and most expensive—salads and vegetables known to earth.

September plants her garden in raised beds, and in preparation for our Mother's Day ritual, she would sometimes request my help in building an addition to her raised-bed garden fortress. And I would gladly make a Saturday-before-Mother's-Day trek to our local building-supply store to buy sundry lumber, soil, compost, hardware, and fencing. Such was the case one fine Saturday-before-Mother's-Day some years ago. With my garden-fortress-improvement list in hand, I climbed into her minivan to head to Home Depot. As I started the car, I noticed a signal that, in my experience, is ever-present in my wife's motor vehicles (see image below).

My wife's fuel tank whenever I borrow her car.

I cannot name the origin of September's inability to win her battle against the little orange gas light, but for whatever reason—perhaps some childhood trauma in a filling station or a rare allergy to fossil fuels—she seems incapable of keeping her gas tank out of the red zone. Maybe it's just me, but the days when her car is sucking fumes seem remarkably aligned to the days when I want to borrow her car. I, on the other hand, and this may not surprise you, break out in a cold sweat if my fuel gauge dips below a quarter of a tank. This is one of the many ways September and I are different.

We joke about this today, but I'm embarrassed to admit that in our early marriage, I was prone to over-protecting whenever I borrowed her car and it was on empty. In short, I was often a jerk. The empty gas tank fueled (pardon the pun) many negative comments from me, and more than a few eye rolls.

But on the day in question, something very different happened. As my typically impatient and self-righteous response rose up, I got a strong prompting, clear as a bell: "Don't make a big deal about this. Just help out your wife and put gas in her car. It's almost Mother's Day, for Pete's sake!" This was my prompting to do something right and good.

I had no confusion here. My List 1 people would not have made a big deal about the gas light being on. They would have cheerfully headed for a gas station and filled up their spouse's car, or in the case of my List 1 hero, George Washington, perhaps fed his wife's horse. And when they returned home, they wouldn't feel the need to point out their good deed.

I wish I could report that I complied with the clear prompting, filled up my wife's gas tank, and set us up for the best Mother's Day ever. But this Saturday morning, I experienced another of my long list of self-deception failures. I ignored the prompting. How did I move so quickly from feeling all tender and loving toward my wife as I set out to help her have a great Mother's Day, to failing to comply with this simple prompting to gas up her car?

Stretching self-deception looks something like this: I get the prompting to do something right and good, and immediately I'm confronted with a choice:

- Do I obey the prompting and feel *satisfied*? or
- Do I ignore the prompting, and then tell distorted stories about September and myself, to feel *justified*?

As soon as we ignore a prompting, we subconsciously begin to tell self-justifying distortions to ease our guilt. We create these twisted stories to let ourselves off the hook for failing to do something we know is right and good. In the stretching style of self-deception, our self-justifying stories make the other person seem worse than they really are and ourselves better than we really are.

In the minivan that Saturday, I immediately started telling self-justifying distortions about my wife, making her seem worse than she really was, to justify my poor choice:

- *She should learn to manage her vehicle like a grown-up.*
- *I'm always filling up her car.*
- *She was running errands all day yesterday; she had plenty of time to put gas in her car.*
- *Wait a minute. She knew I would be taking her car out today . . . I bet she left the tank empty* on purpose.

Notice the theme in all the distortions I made about September: they *accused* her.

And it doesn't stop there. When we deploy stretching self-deception, we also tell self-justifying distortions that make ourselves seem better than we really are. In the minivan that Saturday, I told self-justifying distortions that helped me feel that I was better than I really was:

- *I always keep my gas tank full.*
- *I don't expect her to fill up my gas tank all the time.*
- *I'm really busy today.*
- *I don't want to encourage September's irresponsibility by becoming one of those gas-tank enablers.*

Notice the theme in all the distortions I made about myself: they *excused* me.

This is an important observation. When we deploy stretching self-deception, we embed two themes inside the distorted stories: accuse and excuse. We *accuse* the other person and *excuse* ourselves. These themes partner together to allow us to feel justified and let ourselves off the hook for failing to do something right and good.

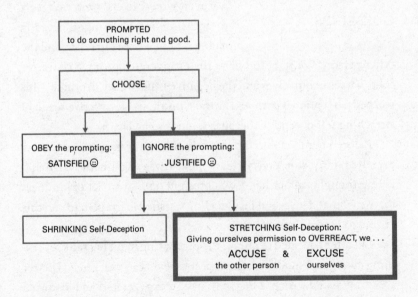

How can you tell if you've slipped into the stretching style of self-deception? Ask yourself, *Am I telling stories that accuse the other person and excuse myself?* If the answer is yes, it's a telltale sign that you're entering the realm of stretching self-deception.

Think about the last time you had a hard conversation with someone. While the other person was talking, were you listening, seeking to understand? Or were you thinking of what you'd say to accuse them while forming excuses for yourself? Did some of the words or phrases you were thinking distort reality in subtle or not-so-subtle ways? Did they help you feel better about yourself? Chances are, at least to some extent, you've found clever ways to use stretching self-deception by accusing the other person and excusing yourself.

WHEN WE DEPLOY STRETCHING SELF-DECEPTION, WE . . . *ACCUSE* THE OTHER PERSON AND *EXCUSE* OURSELVES.

If this were the end of it, that would be bad enough, but when we self-deceive in this manner, things can get even worse. Every time we resort to accusing and excusing, it actually changes how we see ourselves and the other person. We start to *believe* the exaggerated positive character traits we see in ourselves and the negative traits we see in others. This warped perception is perhaps the most insidious, destructive result of stretching self-deception, because it tends to be lasting.

Before I climbed into the minivan that Saturday morning, I saw myself and my wife pretty clearly, and I was filled with warm and loving thoughts about her. I was prompted to do an act of kindness for the woman I love, and I was feeling satisfied in my plan to run this errand to Home Depot for her.

But after I decided to ignore the prompting to fill her tank, everything changed. I suddenly reinterpreted reality in order to feel better about my bad decision. I began to assign exaggerated and distorted negative character traits to September. Suddenly my sweet wife became lazy, selfish, inconsiderate, manipulative, and downright sneaky, so much so that it would be wrong of me to help her out by filling her tank.

Then I began to tell a distorted story about myself, one that ignored the fact that I had just made a selfish choice. I wasn't merely a nice husband running a helpful errand; I somehow became a long-suffering, hardworking, servant-oriented, responsible, and fair husband. I exaggerated my good traits such that I probably deserved a medal, a superhero cape, or maybe even a crown.

AFTER STRETCHING
SELF-DECEPTION: NOT PUTTING
GAS IN SEPTEMBER'S MINIVAN[2]

HOW I SEE SEPTEMBER	HOW I SEE MYSELF
lazy	hardworking
inconsiderate	long-suffering
manipulative	servant-oriented
irresponsible	responsible
sneaky	fair

Do you see how messed up stretching self-deception can be? I ignored a prompting to do something right and good, told distorted stories about myself and my wife, and somehow in the end, my wife became the bad guy and I became the good guy.

Sometimes when I share this gas-tank story while teaching a workshop, someone will come to me afterward and say, "That's all fine and good. I've met your wife and she's amazing. She's not lazy, selfish, or any of those things on your list. But what if *my* spouse actually *is* all those things? What do I do then?" Fair question.

Sooner or later we all experience conflict with people who really are behaving badly. And it's true that there are times when we need to set boundaries and protect ourselves from those people. (I discuss this much more in later chapters.) But we're not responsible for the behavior of others. We're only responsible for our own behavior. It's the only thing we have control over. We can significantly improve our relationships by taking full responsibility for our part of the equation, and we must do so before we can know whether boundary setting or bridge building is our next step.

Even if my wife really was lazy, selfish, and inconsiderate, I still had a prompting to do something right and good, and my choice to ignore this prompting was a mistake, regardless of her character. In order to feel okay with my choice to ignore an internal urge to do something right and good, I needed to imagine my wife as *more* lazy, *more* selfish, and *more* inconsiderate than she really was, all to escape the reality that I wasn't behaving like a List 1 person. Even if September had her own issues, I still *exaggerated* the gap.

When we exaggerate the gap, we warp reality by overlooking the truth that we reacted poorly toward the other person. Responding to my wife's empty gas tank by filling up her car that morning would have demonstrated the ideal levels of accepting and protecting. But because I didn't feel like putting gas in her car, I told stories that somehow allowed me to over-protect and feel justified in doing so.

A Story from the Home Front: The Merging-into-Traffic Cheater

Similarly, despite the small victory in the traffic-merging scenario I mentioned earlier, I've sensed plenty of other promptings to let some poor soul merge into traffic ahead of me but then proceeded to tailgate the car in front of me so closely that I forced the out-of-luck sap in my side mirror to apply his brakes and file in behind me. And whenever I ignore these promptings, I jump into my go-to mode of stretching self-deception and tell self-justifying stories. I accuse the other driver while excusing myself, and I exaggerate to bolster my case. (See the table on the next page.)

When we react with stretching self-deception, we over-protect and overreact; and when we overreact, we make matters worse, widen the gap, and cause greater destruction to our relationships. This all happens in a split second, and often subconsciously. We tell increasingly distorted stories until we convince ourselves that we're doing the right thing, even though we're not. We mute the conviction we feel for not doing something right and good.

PROMPTING: LET THE MERGING-INTO-TRAFFIC CHEATER IN AHEAD OF ME

ACCUSE	EXCUSE
"He should've planned ahead."	"I never cut people off in traffic like this guy."
"He should've put his blinker on sooner."	"I'm in a hurry and don't have time to slow down."
"He's speeding up and not taking his turn."	"I didn't notice him in time."
"Didn't he learn in kindergarten not to cut in line?"	"I don't want to slam on my brakes and trip up the person behind me."
"What a cheater! I bet he does this all the time."	"I already let one car merge in front of me. Doesn't this guy know the 1:1 rule?"
"A guy like this wouldn't let others merge in front of him. I'm just giving him a taste of his own medicine."	"I don't want to be a doormat and let this guy take advantage of me."

When we distort the gap through the stretching style of self-deception, we move too quickly to setting a boundary with others (like not allowing the other driver in ahead of us), rather than building a bridge (waving the driver in). In all cases of stretching self-deception, distorting the gap keeps us from being a List 1 person who consistently lives out those List 2 character traits we so admire.

If you're starting to worry that the ensuing chapters will not help you hold a misbehaving person accountable by setting boundaries, fear not. I'm not suggesting that we should be punching bags or let others walk all over us. I'm simply saying that we must accurately define the problem before we decide our best response to relational disappointments. This process of right-sizing the gaps in our lives helps us get clear on what our next move should be, whether to set a boundary or to build a bridge. But the more prolonged and established our relational disappointment toward another person, the more prone we will be to exaggerate the gap through stretching self-deception.

One Caveat: The Difference Between Nice and Good

"Nice" isn't the same as "right and good." Sometimes the right and good response to a situation is to be strong, truthful, and self-protective, not just nice. Sometimes being right and good means standing up for ourselves and addressing ongoing patterns of bad behavior in other people, or letting them experience the natural consequences of their own behavior rather than rescuing them or giving in to them yet again. Enabling destructive behavior is never right or good; it causes harm to the other person and to us.

No doubt your List 1 people would be comfortable refusing to meet a request that would allow someone's bad behavior to continue. Doing what's right and good means standing up for what we know is best, even if it's uncomfortable or goes against someone else's desires for how we should respond.

Sometimes we face situations where the other person is behaving in an unproductive or destructive manner, and we're prompted *not* to help, indulge, or engage that person. We sense that if our courageous, integrity-driven List 1 people were in this same situation, they would resist, speak up, or stand up for themselves—and we should do the same.

Unfortunately, sometimes in these situations we choose a different response. Sometimes we lack the skills or courage to let someone experience the adverse consequences of their own behavior. When we fail to obey these types of promptings, we're guilty of the other style of self-deception: shrinking self-deception.

Shrinking Self-Deception

The distorted stories we tell when we use the shrinking style of self-deception also make us feel better about ourselves and our bad choices. But in these cases, instead of exaggerating the gap by making the other person worse than they really are (and ourselves better than we are), we minimize the gap by making the situation less problematic than it really is. The shrinking style of self-deception tells self-justifying stories that downplay the problem and justify our lack of action. For example, no matter how awfully the other person behaved, we tell ourselves:

- *It's not that big a deal.*
- *It could have been so much worse.*
- *The next time this happens, then I'll do something about it.*

This lets us off the hook from having to respond in a right and good way, which probably means a stronger and more protecting response.

When we use shrinking self-deception, we give ourselves permission *not* to take responsibility, *not* to take action, or *not* to deal with our disappointment "this time." We stay in the comfy bridge-building mode, even though setting a boundary would be more productive in the long run. We over-accept, under-protect, and therefore, underreact.

> THE SHRINKING STYLE OF SELF-DECEPTION TELLS SELF-JUSTIFYING STORIES THAT DOWNPLAY THE PROBLEM AND JUSTIFY OUR LACK OF ACTION.

There are two telltale strategies within shrinking self-deception: minimizing and rationalizing. (See the chart on the next page.)

Minimize the Problem

When we minimize, we pretend the issue is smaller than it really is so we're not forced to take protective action. We emphasize the importance of accepting the other person rather than protecting ourselves.

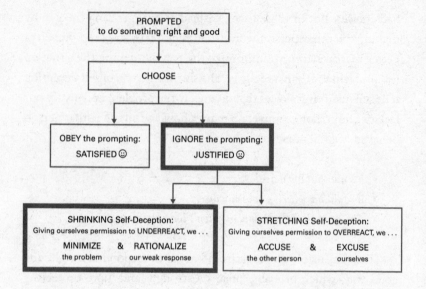

We're more comfortable maintaining a status quo in the relationship rather than setting a firm boundary. As a result, we continue carrying the negative consequences of the other person's behavior, failing to see the potential destruction our passivity wreaks on ourselves and on the other person in the long run.

One clue that we're minimizing is when we use the phrase, "At least" at the beginning of a phrase to justify our lack of action and explain how the problem isn't really that bad. Here are a few examples:

At least . . .
- "She doesn't do it on purpose."
- "He doesn't hit me."
- "She's not using *hard* drugs."
- "He doesn't yell in public."
- "She's still getting good grades."
- "He's still a great dad to the kids."
- "She's a good provider."

- "His bark is worse than his bite."
- "She only does it on weekends."
- "He only drinks at home."
- "I still have a job."
- "It's only money."
- "He always says he's sorry afterward."

Rationalize Our Weak Response

When we rationalize, we paint the problem as being less in our power to influence, or as less of our personal responsibility. The phrases we often use begin with, "Yes, but . . ."

Here are some examples of phrases someone might use to rationalize their weak response to a problem:

Yes, but . . .
- "All the men in his family have anger problems."
- "She had a rough childhood."
- "He's a strong-willed child."
- "My boss is under a lot of stress."
- "He'll grow out of it."
- "She promised she'll never do it again."
- "If I confront him, it'll just make matters worse."
- "I know that I can be needy too."
- "The kids make her so mad."
- "He only does this when he drinks."
- "She has a lot of baggage at home."
- "What goes around comes around. Someday this will catch up with him."
- "I'm better off without her anyways."
- "Now isn't a good time. I'll deal with it next time."
- "He's doing his best."
- "My therapist says I need to avoid adding stress to my life right now."

- "I don't want to hurt or embarrass her by sharing my disappointment."

My friend Steve works as a middle manager in a large international company. He came to see me about an increased tension he feels at work because of his new boss. He inadvertently came across a potential problem in a new policy the boss had introduced that, if left unchanged, would put the company at risk for claiming hundreds of thousands of dollars of tax write-offs, which Steve is convinced would be illegal. Alarmed at the implications of this policy, and assuming it was an unintentional oversight, Steve took his discovery to his new boss. He expected the boss to be impressed and grateful for such a careful observation, but what he experienced was the opposite.

"Keep your nose in your own business," the boss told him. "Maybe you should just trust that I know more than you about standard practices in these areas and leave the accounting to the accountants."

To his dismay, Steve realized that the new boss was not only aware of this indiscretion but had instituted the new policy with this sketchy benefit in mind. This situation was particularly tricky because even though he was not an accountant, his role included entering the erroneous new code on all his expense reports. He knew, deep down, that this was wrong, and likely illegal.

Steve tends to be more of an acceptor than a protector, more of a bridge builder than a boundary setter. His patient, easygoing personality is actually one of his best qualities and the reason people love and appreciate him. However, as such, he's prone to be a people pleaser. As a natural bridge builder, he more often deploys the shrinking style of distorting stories, rather than the stretching style. As is common with all of us facing a situation like this, he was tempted to self-deceive.

I listened to him verbally process his difficult situation for some time. It sounded like this:

MINIMIZE	RATIONALIZE
At least . . .	Yes, but . . .
• "My boss isn't stealing from the customer."	• "Apparently, this behavior is normal in our industry."
• "It only impacts 15 percent of our inventory."	• "I'm just following my boss's orders."
• "We're still paying most of our taxes."	• "My boss's solution is still better than moving the company offshore to avoid taxes."
• "Our company pays millions in taxes to the government already."	

I could tell by the look on Steve's face that he wasn't proud of the words coming out of his mouth. He's a man of character, and it was clear that at some level he wasn't buying his own words and was being prompted to do something right and good in this hard situation. But like all of us facing a gap in an important relationship, he was finding it difficult to get clarity on both his reality and his desire. What he desired was an honest boss who appreciated his attention to detail. But reality looked quite different, and he was beginning to distort the gap by minimizing his boss's behavior (making the issue smaller than it actually was) and rationalizing his own lack of response thus far (lessening his personal responsibility for the problem).

The two of us talked through the paradigm of shrinking versus stretching self-deception, and Steve identified that his natural bent was toward creating shrinking stories that helped him ignore promptings to do what is right and good in his current situation.

"Dang," he said, grinning and shaking his head. "With my boss, I'm minimizing and rationalizing."

Steve knew he had some hard decisions to make. Whether he decides to confront his boss more assertively, take this issue to a higher level of management, or change jobs altogether is up to him, but I was impressed with his integrity, and his commitment to obey promptings to do right and good things, even at a personal sacrifice.

OVERACHIEVERS: USING BOTH STRETCHING AND SHRINKING STYLES OF SELF-DECEPTION

We've covered a lot of ground thus far, and introduced a lot of new terms, all in an effort to understand ourselves and our risks for self-deception.

While it's true that, in general, we're more apt to accuse and excuse when we're using stretching self-deception and minimize and rationalize when we're deploying shrinking self-deception, many of us have become such experts at telling self-justifying stories that we often use all four of these strategies—accuse, excuse, minimize, and rationalize—in the same situation, regardless of whether we're trying to make the gap seem larger or smaller.

Such was the case with Daniel, a guy who came by my office to talk about some struggles he was having in his marriage. Daniel is a fairly self-aware guy who knows he sometimes resorts to shrinking self-deception as his go-to strategy in conflicts. His nine-year marriage to Audrey hasn't been the easiest, but in the past couple of years, she has become increasingly demanding and controlling.

"Nothing I do seems to help," he said. "Audrey wants all of my time. I no longer have any outside activities that don't involve her, and my only friends are a few acquaintances at work. All my old friends have given up trying to get together with me because Audrey doesn't like it. And I cave under pressure and make up some dumb excuse so I can stay home with her. I just keep trying to please her, and she still isn't satisfied."

Audrey's control, coupled with Daniel's passivity, created the perfect environment for self-deception. In the early days of his marital disappointment, Daniel mostly deployed shrinking self-deception to justify his unwillingness to stand up to his wife. *At least she's a great mom to the kids*, he'd think. Or *Audrey's family of origin is pretty screwed up, so there's not much I can do.* He minimized and rationalized.

Over time, he began to shift his self-deception strategy. "I always tell myself I'm more of a bridge builder," he said. "But there's just no bridge long enough to satisfy my wife. I've tried talking to her about how controlling she can be, but she just can't hear it. She's very defensive. Everyone in her family has control issues. You should meet my mother-in-law! Control is all Audrey knows."

Daniel's passivity only increased their problems, and now he was at a breaking point. "At this point," he said, "I'm just hanging in there for the sake of the kids."

"I'm so sorry to hear all this," I said. "Do you mind if I ask you a hard question?"

"Go ahead," he said. "It can't hurt!"

"Is there a chance that what you're labeling as 'bridge building' might be more accurately defined as people pleasing, conflict avoiding, or codependency?"

He squirmed. "Possibly. I mean, if I weren't so afraid of the aftermath that follows every time I stand up to her, I'd probably try a different strategy instead of just rolling over and giving in to her. Clearly, my current MO isn't working."

My guess is that if Daniel were to think of some List 1 people he admires and then describe their character traits, strength and self-assurance would be among them. If someone's behavior becomes destructive, as was the case with Audrey's insecurity and control, List 1 people know how to shift from accepting someone's behavior to protecting themselves from negative consequences of that behavior by setting boundaries.

As Daniel described his current marriage situation, he used some textbook shrinking self-deception language designed to make the gap appear smaller than it really was. These half-truths helped him justify his lack of action and feel less sheepish about not standing up for himself:

SHRINKING SELF-DECEPTION	
MINIMIZE THE PROBLEM	RATIONALIZE MY LACK OF ACTION
At least . . . • "She's a great mom to the kids." • "She would never cheat on me."	Yes, but . . . • "Everyone in Audrey's family has control issues." • "Control is all Audrey knows."

In addition, Daniel employed some great stretching self-deception language designed to make Audrey worse than she really was, and himself less culpable than he really was. In this case, his distortion describes a problem so big that it's hopeless to try to fix it.

STRETCHING SELF-DECEPTION	
ACCUSE THE OTHER PERSON	EXCUSE MYSELF
• "There's just no bridge long enough to satisfy my wife." • "It's just never enough." • "She's super defensive. She just can't admit to anything she ever did wrong."	• "I've tried everything in my power to please her." • "I've sacrificed so much for Audrey." • "I'm just hanging in there for the sake of the kids."

One reason it's so hard to catch ourselves in self-deception (stretch: accuse/excuse, or shrink: minimize/rationalize) is that our self-justifying stories typically hold nuggets of truth, making them easier to swallow and leaving most of the responsibility for the problem in the hands of the other person.

In Daniel's case, Audrey has a controlling mom, she is almost certainly defensive, and it's likely that Daniel has tried talking to her about these issues. Regardless, none of his statements represent the whole truth. And until Daniel gets more honest about accurately defining the gap and chooses a different strategy to manage it, he's unlikely to stop the current unhealthy dance that's destroying his marriage.

I admired Daniel's willingness to face some honest and difficult truths about his own culpability in their marital struggles. Over the nine years of their marriage, he had become a master at using all four strategies for justifying his unproductive responses to his wife. As we talked, he began to define reality with more accuracy (what's *really* going on). He identified how his passivity was a huge part of their unhealthy rhythm. With a more accurate picture of reality and a renewed sense of his desire to heal and grow his marriage (what do I *really* want), Daniel found the confidence he needed to set some reasonable boundaries with Audrey.

I'm not proud to admit this, but I, too, can be an overachiever when it comes to self-deception. In the case of my prompting to fill September's gas tank, I deftly defended my decision not to fill up her tank by accusing and excusing, but inside I also minimized: "At least I'm only driving a few miles. It won't take that much gas." And I rationalized: "I had no way of knowing the car would be empty when I budgeted time for this trip."

And in my traffic-merging episodes, I can quickly rattle off some accuse-and-excuse lines to defend my overreaction to marauding motorists. I can minimize: "Yes, but someone else will let him in. It's not that big a deal to let him wait." And I can rationalize: "He created his problem, so he needs to solve it."

How about you? Are you a self-deception overachiever? Are you able to wield expertise in all four distortion strategies? Most of us can. Until we become aware of our tendencies, we'll stay trapped in the harmful patterns of accuse, excuse, minimize, and rationalize, and consistently fail to demonstrate the character traits of the List 1 people we so admire.

Back to the Story of Mary and Will: What's Really Going On?

Remember Mary and her husband Will, the guy who had back surgery and wasn't carrying his weight financially or with the kids?

During our last conversation, Mary had gained clarity about her desire and what she *really* wanted in her relationship with Will: she wanted her loving life partner and teammate back. After leaving my office, she pursued counseling and found a therapist she really liked. I checked in on her progress.

In my very first conversation with Mary, I'd listened to the full brunt of her dissatisfaction with Will and the state of their marriage. I'd watched her transition from shrinking to stretching self-deception, which is quite common when someone's pain gets high enough.

In describing the early years of Will's unemployment, Mary was operating from the left side of the accepting/protecting (A/P) spectrum and was over-accepting. In that season, she had used some classic shrinking self-deception language to describe her situation:

MARY'S SHRINKING STYLE OF SELF-DECEPTION WITH WILL	
MINIMIZE THE PROBLEM	RATIONALIZE MY LACK OF ACTION
At least . . .	Yes, but . . .
• "He's nice to me and the kids." • "He's not addicted to all those pain meds the doctor prescribed." • "He's not addicted to *illegal* drugs." • "He doesn't hit me."	• "He can't help that his back is injured." • "Those idiots at Will's job never even gave him a chance." • "Those pain meds make him really tired. He just has no energy to look for work."

Notice how Mary amped up her shrinking self-deception as the situation with Will grew worse. And then when her frustrations reached a boiling point, she made a dramatic swing from shrinking self-deception (minimize/rationalize) to stretching self-deception (accuse/excuse). She moved from the left side of the A/P spectrum to the right side, where she found herself dangerously over-protecting: she became harsh with Will and wanted out of the marriage.

By exaggerating the problem instead of minimizing it, Mary felt justified in throwing in the towel, which was her first step in defending herself. See how she used classic stretching self-deception language as she accused Will and excused herself:

MARY'S STRETCHING STYLE OF SELF-DECEPTION	
ACCUSE THE OTHER PERSON	**EXCUSE MYSELF**
Accuse Will	Excuse herself
• "I've been reading some books on personality types, and I'm pretty sure Will is a narcissist." • "Will is a deadbeat dad. If he really loved the kids, he wouldn't have missed so many of Brittany's soccer games."	• "I've done all I can to save our marriage." • "I've been too patient and loving for too long." • "I'm through with this marriage. And who could blame me?"

Mary stopped by my office after several months of working with her therapist. I was surprised to see her upbeat and smiling.

Mary: Well, you'll be proud. Will and I are each seeing therapists.

Me: Great news! I'm truly impressed. And how's that going?

Mary: Well, at first, my therapist ticked me off. She had *the nerve* to suggest I might have contributed somewhat to our marriage problems. She wanted me to do "my work" first. I told her, "*My* work? But I'm not the deadbeat narcissist here!"

We both laughed, because she and I know that every relational conflict has two combatants, no matter how one-sided it might look from the outside. Mary was clearly open to exploring her contributions, and already I could see hope in her eyes. This was a courageous woman.

Mary: At my first counseling session, I gave my poor therapist an earful about how awful Will is and how much of a victim I was. Then she asked me to describe the family I grew up in, which seemed weird. I told her I wasn't having conflict with my family!

Me: Wise therapist. We all learn how relationships work during those early years of our childhood, so it's important to understand what was normal for you in your family of origin.

Mary: She promised me she'd tie this into my marriage problems, so I humored her.

Mary spent the next several minutes giving me a snapshot of the environment of her childhood home. She was the oldest of four kids, born to middle-class Midwestern parents. But then, when Mary was five, her dad ran off to California with a neighbor woman. "And my mother never recovered," she said. By the time Mary reached elementary school, her mother was stressed and bitter. By junior high, her mom had become depressed and demanding, expecting Mary to essentially raise her younger children for her. Mary began surrendering many of her own school activities and friendships to care for her siblings and her mom.

As she shared this part of her story, her eyes filled with tears. "I spent my whole childhood trying to please and cheer up my mom by caring for everyone else," she said. "Now I'm married to someone who doesn't help at home and demands my care too. It's like a sick déjà vu."

As you read Mary's story, can you see some pieces falling into place with how she responds to Will? Her lifelong pattern of trying to please and care for others has come at a high cost to her own needs and desires. Her childhood pattern of compliance and self-sacrifice affected more than just her marriage. It affected all her relationships. At work, her abusive boss consistently expected

Mary to take on extra projects, stay late for last-minute tasks, and finish other people's work. And she would do so. At her kids' school, people on her Parent, Teacher, and Student Association (PTSA) team frequently neglected to follow through with their commitments, knowing Mary would pick up the slack. And she silently complied.

The coping skills Mary learned as a child were no longer serving her well as an adult. As is true for many of us, the defense mechanisms that helped us survive disappointments and painful circumstances as kids or teens don't help us develop healthy relationships as adults. Mary had become an expert at helping, pleasing, and complying with her mom's demands. And she brought those same tools into her marriage and work.

Mary: With my boss or the PTSA team, I get passive-aggressive. I make myself scarce around the office and stop responding to texts, or I just suck it up and do the extra stuff so I don't disappoint them. But with Will, it's different. I've become controlling and negative toward him, like my mom was toward me.

Me: What does that look like? What does Will see when you get that way?

THE DEFENSE MECHANISMS THAT HELPED US SURVIVE DISAPPOINTMENTS AND PAINFUL CIRCUMSTANCES AS KIDS OR TEENS DON'T HELP US DEVELOP HEALTHY RELATIONSHIPS AS ADULTS.

Mary: If I'm honest, I've been pretty critical of Will, even before he hurt his back. His job, his friends, his hobbies, his diet. . . . And over these past couple of years, the poor guy couldn't do anything right in my eyes. Then he got injured, and I just resented being the one who always had to do everything.

Me: We both agree Will has some work to do. But maybe you have some work to do too.

Mary: True. Sounds fun.

Me: Nope, not fun. But liberating, and worth the effort. When we respond to our disappointment in helpful ways, we create an environment that allows both parties to behave in mutually respectful and benevolent ways. You can't control Will, but you can control how you respond to him. You can stop using the outdated tools that served you well as a child. And you can start letting Will carry the consequences for his own destructive behavior.

Being overly accepting and people pleasing undoubtedly contributed to Mary's dysfunctional relationship with Will. Her lifelong pattern of being the person in the relationship who always capitulates, performs, and sacrifices took its toll. Over time her resentment grew, and then leaked out, bringing further damage to her marriage. She hit a wall and shifted from shrinking self-deception (people pleasing with resentment) to stretching self-deception ("Will's a narcissist and I want a divorce").

Over months in therapy, Mary came to realize that she had never discovered her own voice as a child, and so hadn't developed the skills of communicating her needs and standing up for herself in relationships. She began to recognize that the same unhealthy relational pattern repeatedly manifested itself in her life: Whenever someone important to her—Will, her mother, her daughter, or her boss—places unreasonable expectations on her, she fears that if she doesn't comply, she'll disappoint them and possibly end up abandoned or rejected. She capitulates without voicing her own needs. And over time, her resentment builds until it leaks out, making the relationships even more unrewarding and toxic.

Once Mary spotted this pattern in her adult life, a light bulb went off. She'd always assumed she just seemed to attract unreasonable people and toxic relationships. But now she realized she actually contributed to the toxicity through her people pleasing and passivity. Her tendency to over-accept other peoples' expectations rather than use her voice and protect herself actively contributed to her relationship problems—especially with Will.

Mary's understanding of the question, What's *really* going on? had deepened, and she saw a more accurate assessment of reality, which included her contributions to their problems:

WILL'S CONTRIBUTIONS	MARY'S CONTRIBUTIONS
• He isn't making any financial contributions to the household. • He provides minimal parenting support for their three children and does little to help with the running of their household. • He is emotionally distant and uncommunicative, leaving Mary lonely for her life partner and teammate.	• Throughout their marriage, she failed to be clear, kind, and courageous in communicating her needs and desires; her indirectness sent Will mixed messages. • In the past several years, she flipped from being a passive people pleaser to an aggressive critic. • She has become bitter about her role as a people pleaser, and her resentment is now leaking onto Will.

We have tremendous power to change the unhealthy dance we're in, even if nothing changes in the other person's behavior. When we clarify the gap and then temper our responses with ideal amounts of accepting and protecting, we maximize the odds of narrowing the gap and finding greater relational satisfaction.

As we prepare to dive into the nuts and bolts of boundary setting, think of a current gap you're experiencing in an important relationship. Seek insight with humility and honesty as you clarify the gap. Where are you minimizing the problem or rationalizing your weak response? Where are you accusing the other person and excusing yourself? Take ownership for your contribution to the relational disappointment. In doing so, you move one step closer to being like the List 1 people you admire.

PART III

Protecting: How to
Set a Boundary

WHERE WE'RE HEADED:

- The tasks *before* the boundary-setting conversation
- The tasks *during* the boundary-setting conversation
- The tasks *after* the boundary-setting conversation

Congratulations! By engaging in the first two parts of this book, you've taken a deep dive into understanding relational disappointments—the gap between our desires and reality—and the dual strategies of accepting and protecting.

You've done the hard work of defining the gap. You're convinced there is a problem and that something must change. You want to renovate your relationship. And now you have clarity on which ingredient (accepting or protecting) you need to add to the relationship to reach an ideal balance.

If, on the other hand, you turned to this page because you scanned the Table of Contents and thought chapter 8 contained the meat of the book, I beg you, go back and start from the beginning. The information in parts I and II offers you the greatest hope of making helpful strides in your relationships. Without the foundational concepts found in those chapters, you'll likely misdiagnose your relationship and then use the information in chapters 8 and beyond to apply the wrong solutions.

At this stage in the book, you've worked your way from the top toward the bottom of the *Renovate Your Relationships Pathway* chart (see below), and you have accomplished some important tasks. You've refrained from making things worse, and you right-sized the gap by answering two questions: What's *really* going on? and What do I *really* want?

RENOVATE YOUR RELATIONSHIPS PATHWAY

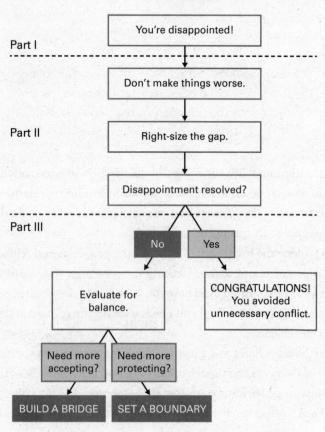

So far so good. With a sober view of the situation, you're equipped to discern the ideal combination of accepting and protecting to apply to your disappointment. You can refresh your memory of our work from chapter 2 by taking a look at the *Accepting/Protecting (A/P) Spectrum* diagram below:

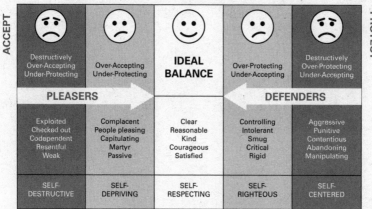

ACCEPTING/PROTECTING (A/P) SPECTRUM				
Destructively Over-Accepting Under-Protecting	Over-Accepting Under-Protecting	**IDEAL BALANCE**	Over-Protecting Under-Accepting	Destructively Over-Protecting Under-Accepting
PLEASERS →			← DEFENDERS	
Exploited Checked out Codependent Resentful Weak	Complacent People pleasing Capitulating Martyr Passive	Clear Reasonable Kind Courageous Satisfied	Controlling Intolerant Smug Critical Rigid	Aggressive Punitive Contentious Abandoning Manipulating
SELF-DESTRUCTIVE	SELF-DEPRIVING	SELF-RESPECTING	SELF-RIGHTEOUS	SELF-CENTERED

ACCEPT / PROTECT

If, after right-sizing your gap, you sense you're still living on the right side of the spectrum by over-protecting, I invite you to go back and review chapter 3, which highlights how to respond with more accepting.

But the vast majority of readers will find themselves on the left side of the spectrum, on the over-accepting side. If this describes you, your situation requires more protecting, and it's time to set a boundary.

The remainder of this book walks you through the nuts and bolts of how to increase the protecting proportion in your responses; that is, how to set a boundary. In this part III, we'll explore the process of setting a boundary through the three movements of before, during, and after the boundary-setting conversation.

EIGHT

BEFORE THE CONVERSATION

WHERE WE'RE HEADED:

The tasks *before* the boundary-setting conversation:

1. Secure a safe, stable support system
2. Remember what a boundary is *not*
3. Name the troubling behavior and its consequence
4. Decide on boundaries that are clear, kind, and courageous
5. Anticipate reactions and risks

When we find ourselves squarely on the left side of the accepting/protecting (A/P) spectrum, where we're over-accepting and under-protecting and we've tried building bridges to no avail, it's time to set a boundary.

How do we get started? An often-quoted piece of old agricultural wisdom says, "If I had six hours to chop down a tree, I would spend the first four sharpening the axe."[1] This axiom speaks to the point of this chapter: preparation matters. When faced with an important or weighty task, taking time to properly prepare is key to success. And preparation is vital when it comes to having a boundary-setting conversation with someone important to us. The time we invest *before* the actual conversation will set us up for success, no matter how the other person chooses to respond.

This chapter details the five critical tasks that need to take place before you engage the other person in a boundary-setting conversation.

1. SECURE A SAFE, STABLE SUPPORT SYSTEM

If a pattern of over-accepting and under-protecting with a loved one is long-standing or severe, we may find ourselves somewhat isolated from other friends or supportive relatives. The destructive behavior of the other person may have chased them away, or perhaps out of our own embarrassment over our messy situation we have distanced ourselves. As a result, when we finally come to the conclusion that we need to make changes in the relationship, too often we don't have a safe, stable support system waiting nearby to help us. We're alone, and that's scary.

Because the process of setting boundaries often requires breaking old patterns, facing the fear of disappointing others, and tackling self-doubt, it's essential to have safe and wise people supporting us *throughout* the boundary-setting journey. Ideally, this includes a mixture of friends, family, coworkers, and professionals. If your current relationship has left you isolated, and the boundary you're about to set is significant, I strongly recommend you find

> BECAUSE THE PROCESS OF SETTING BOUNDARIES OFTEN REQUIRES BREAKING OLD PATTERNS, FACING THE FEAR OF DISAPPOINTING OTHERS, AND TACKLING SELF-DOUBT, IT'S ESSENTIAL TO HAVE SAFE AND WISE PEOPLE SUPPORTING US *THROUGHOUT* THE BOUNDARY-SETTING JOURNEY.

both a licensed therapist and at least one same-gender friend or family member to be your safe people.

What makes someone a safe person in your life? Their ability to both support and protect you, and to speak wise, honest words to you. This isn't the time to surround yourself with people who just cheer you on or indulge your venting or whining. While commiserating has its place, you need courageous, truthful friends who can help you see your situation clearly. They can help you recalibrate when you over-accept/over-protect or react in a way that makes things worse. Your safe, stable support team should demonstrate the balance of expressing both grace and truth in your life.

If you proceed in setting a boundary without first securing a stable support system, you substantially increase the risk of falling back into old patterns or overreacting and making things worse. Invest the time to find at least two safe people who can support you.

Once you have a few people in mind, bring them up to speed on your situation and your need to set a boundary. Ask for their input:

- What blind spots can they help you see?
- What differing point of view would be helpful to hear?
- What insight can they offer to help you right-size your gap between reality (what's *really* going on) and desire (what do you *really* want)?
- What's your contribution to this situation? Are you fully owning it?
- Is the boundary you plan to set designed to protect you or to try to control or change the other person?

2. REMEMBER WHAT A BOUNDARY IS *NOT*

Remember, boundaries are defense, not offense. A good boundary keeps adverse consequences with the rightful owner.

Sometimes the adverse consequences of someone's behavior are clear and uncomplicated. For example, a man with an anger problem owns the consequences of his raging, such as a lost job, lost friendships, or embarrassment when he loses his temper in public. But his family lives with fear and anxiety in their own home. The tense, unsafe home environment is the adverse consequence of his raging.

Other times, adverse consequences can be harder to name. For example, someone who habitually lies might leave a varied trail of adverse consequences in their wake. If you're in a relationship with someone who fudges the truth, it may take some work to discern the specific adverse consequences you want to transfer back on them. If the liar is a coworker, and the consequence of her lying is lost sales due to clients' lack of trust, you may decide you're no longer willing to partner with her on your accounts. If the liar is your spouse and the dishonesty is related to spending, perhaps you'll choose to split your finances into two checking accounts.

The key here is to regularly remind yourself that your primary goal in boundary setting isn't to change the other person; it's to protect yourself from that person's behavior. Before I increase the amount of protecting in my response to someone, I try to discipline myself to ask the question, "Am I trying to manipulate, coerce, or punish this person with this action, or am I truly focused on leaving the natural consequence of the behavior with its rightful owner?" This question serves as a great litmus test for our motivations before we proceed toward a boundary-setting conversation.

3. NAME THE TROUBLING BEHAVIOR AND ITS CONSEQUENCE

Regardless of the details of your situation, you'll need to be clear and specific with the other person about the behavior they're exhibiting and the consequences you're experiencing as a result of that behavior, so they understand exactly what you're no longer willing to carry. In preparation for the conversation, spend some time getting clear on the specific consequence you are returning to its rightful owner. Naming the troubling consequence means stating a two-part fact that both parties can agree on:

undesired behavior of the other person + adverse consequences that you've been carrying

Craft your statement carefully, so you don't pollute it with subjective emotions or opinions against which the other person will want to argue. And don't minimize or soft-pedal the behavior that is causing the consequence you're no longer willing to carry. Just state the two-part fact clearly in a single sentence, like this:

- "When you yell and rage at me and the kids, we feel anxious and afraid."
- "Your dishonesty with customers cost us three accounts last month, which ate into my commission by almost 50 percent."
- "Your overspending emptied our checking account last month and we bounced two checks when I paid the bills."

4. DECIDE ON BOUNDARIES THAT ARE CLEAR, KIND, AND COURAGEOUS

Once you've gotten clarity on the adverse consequence you're no longer willing to carry for another person, it's time to clearly and specifically craft the boundary you plan to set. How will you respond the next time the troubling behavior shows itself? What exactly will you do to keep the adverse consequence out of your lap and in the lap of its rightful owner, where it belongs?

Being specific is key. If your boundary statement is fuzzy or vague, you're likely to cause misunderstanding. The resulting confusion could increase conflict, sabotage your boundary, and leave you at risk of reverting back to status quo, or worse. Whether the other person's behavior is mildly troubling or wildly destructive, it's only fair that you communicate your "new day" in the relationship with great detail, so all parties know exactly what to expect should the behavior continue. State your specific boundary in a kind, clear, and courageous voice. (More on this in chapter 9.)

Imagine you want to set a boundary with someone who is unkind and harsh toward you. That person's hurtful, belittling words often get spoken in public, leaving you embarrassed. You realize you've been over-accepting this behavior for too long and need to set a boundary.

Here is what you would *not* say: "From now on, when you're not nice, I won't put up with it." This statement is neither clear nor specific. Who gets to decide what constitutes "nice"? What does "not put up with it" look like exactly? The other person is at a loss as to what adverse consequence you are no longer willing to carry, and what will happen if they don't stop. A statement like this will only foster more angst and argument than if you said nothing at all. This isn't setting a boundary.

A vague, nonspecific phrase can cause the following problems:

- It attacks the person, rather than their behavior.
- It fails to describe the troubling behavior clearly.
- It fails to connect the troubling behavior to the negative consequence you're no longer willing to carry.
- It fails to provide clarity on how you'll respond the next time the behavior occurs.

Let's look at each of these problems in more detail.

Vague Phrases Attack the Person, Rather than Their Behavior

The phrase, "you're not nice" criticizes the person, not the person's behavior. Whenever we make negative, blanket statements about someone's character, we trigger a defensive response. And these types of statements will almost always generate protest and resistance. The other person will want to walk us through all the ways they're not what we accuse them of being.

When we criticize the person as opposed to their behavior, we fail to move the conversation or the relationship forward. When describing the behavior that is prompting a boundary, start with the phrase, "The next time you choose to . . . ." This increases the likelihood that you'll outline the behavior, rather than attack the person.

Vague Phrases Fail to Describe the Troubling Behavior Clearly

What does "not nice" mean exactly? Will both of you agree when "not nice" occurs again? Lack of clarity about the undesired behavior creates more tension, argument, and dissonance, not less. Based on someone's cultural background and family of origin, a wide range of behaviors could fall into the "not nice" category. The same is true for most adjectives that describe behavior, such as kind, weak, strong, honoring, angry, submissive, punctual, thoughtful, aggressive, and more. Spelling out the undesired behavior, rather than applying a label, can bypass avoidable tension and make it more likely to have our boundaries honored.

Imagine, again, that you told someone, "From now on, when you're

> WHEN WE CRITICIZE THE PERSON AS OPPOSED TO THEIR BEHAVIOR, WE FAIL TO MOVE THE CONVERSATION OR THE RELATIONSHIP FORWARD.

not nice to me, I won't put up with it." Two days later, that person gets upset because of something you did, rolls their eyes at you, and starts the following conversation:

Them: You're being ridiculous.

You: You just rolled your eyes and called me ridiculous. I warned you about this a couple of days ago. I'm going to set a boundary to protect myself. I'm leaving the room because you're not being nice.

Them: What do you mean, "not nice"?! I'm just defending myself! How are we ever going to work through this problem if you just walk out whenever it gets hard? You're the one who's "not nice."

See how our fuzzy, vague descriptions of the problem behavior and our planned response can actually get us the opposite of what we want? Descriptors that are more specific are more likely to be clearly understood by both parties. For example:

When you choose to . . .
- call me a crude name . . .
- yell at me . . .
- not clean up your dirty dishes . . .
- hit your sister . . .
- demean the kids . . .
- spend money outside of our prearranged budget . . .
- not give me equal opportunity to present reports at the meeting . . .
- talk about me behind my back . . .
- play your music so loudly that the neighbors complain . . .
- come home after curfew without calling . . .
- interrupt me when I'm sharing in group . . .

- talk over me and refuse to listen to my side . . .
- make disparaging comments about me at gatherings . . .
- have more than two drinks at dinner with the family . . .
- look at pornography . . .

While there is still some margin for interpretation in the examples presented—What is "yelling"? What is "pornography"?—confusion or misalignment is far less likely to sabotage your progress when you use clear statements like these.

Let's look at another example of a fuzzy description of troubling behavior: "When you're disrespectful to others . . ." Again, what does "disrespectful" look like? The definition is subjective. Disrespectful according to whom? It's neither clear nor specific. It describes a wide range of reasonable interpretations that can lead to arguing and defensiveness.

Clear and specific phrases to describe "disrespectful" might include:

The next time you choose to . . .
- leave your dirty dishes in the living room . . .
- use a racial slur . . .
- not show up for meetings without calling . . .
- raise your voice or use profanity with others . . .
- refuse to answer when your grandparents ask you a question . . .
- interrupt others when they're speaking . . .
- criticize someone's political views [or dress, vocation, etc.] at family gatherings . . .
- give the finger to other drivers when I'm in the car with you . . .

These phrases leave no uncertainty. The other person will have no doubt when they have crossed the line.

Vague Phrases Fail to Connect the Troubling Behavior to the Negative Consequence You're No Longer Willing to Carry

The reason you're setting boundaries is because the other person's behavior creates consequences that negatively impact you. If you fail to be specific about those consequences, the other person may assume that you're setting boundaries simply to control or manipulate them.

What are those consequences you're no longer willing to carry for someone else? Boundary statements should clearly describe the consequences you plan to protect yourself from, moving forward. We aren't protecting ourselves from the other person's choices: their drinking, yelling, getting fired, arriving late, interrupting, being rude, looking at pornography, and so on. Instead, we're protecting ourselves from the negative consequences their choices cause us, what we experience when they choose those behaviors. We have every right to protect ourselves from abuse, embarrassment, time wasted, worry, emotional harm, risk to our safety, financial distress, and the like.

By clearly stating the consequence—how someone else's behavior affects you—you're helping that person understand that you're not insisting that they stop the behavior, but simply letting them know that you're no longer willing to experience the negative consequence of the behavior.

Here are some examples of consequences stated in clear, specific terms:

When you [insert their troubling behavior],
- you publicly embarrass and demean me.
- our financial future is put at risk.
- it creates an unsafe environment for me and the kids.
- it costs me client revenue.
- I don't get to spend time with the family.
- I spend too much of my vacation in the car.

- I have to do the lion's share of the parenting alone.
- I end up being the one who has to explain it to the kids.
- I must handle all the negative feedback from the neighbors.
- I'm afraid for my safety.

Once you've clearly defined both the troubling behavior and its consequence, it's time to bring clarity to how you'll respond the next time this behavior occurs.

Vague Phrases Fail to Provide Clarity on How You'll Respond the Next Time the Behavior Occurs

If you tell someone, "Next time you [name the troubling behavior], I won't put up with it," then you've only muddied the waters. What does "won't put up with it" mean? What steps will you take if it happens again? How will you respond in that moment? Phrases like these risk sounding like a veiled threat. They won't help the other person understand how you plan to react the next time their behavior adversely impacts you.

If you don't tell someone clearly how you'll respond the next time they violate your boundary, they will almost certainly be surprised and displeased when you suddenly stop being over-accepting of their behavior. And who can blame them? You've changed the rules of your relationship without telling them. It's only fair to give them clear, specific details ahead of time, so they'll know how you'll respond the next time you experience consequences that belong to them. Then, if the troubling behavior occurs again and you enact your new protecting, boundary-setting response, they should not be surprised. You've given them fair warning, and you're now simply following through with your prearranged plan.

Here are examples of clearly stated responses:

The next time you [state the undesired behavior], I will . . .
- leave the meeting.
- take an Uber home.

- open my own checking account and split our finances.
- walk you to your room, where you will stay until dinner; then your sister and I will continue playing the game without the risk of you hitting her.
- take that client account myself and leave you to find your own leads.
- spend my vacation time visiting my family without you.
- buy a plane ticket and meet you there.
- spend the weekend with my parents, where I can get some parenting support.
- tell the kids the full truth if they ask, without lying to protect you.
- begin the meeting without you.
- take the kids and spend the night in a hotel.

If the other person resists or tries to rehash the conversation you already had with them, you can then say with a clear conscience, "I am sad you're disappointed by my response, but we already talked about this, and now I'm simply following through with exactly what I told you I would do the next time you chose to [state their troubling behavior]."

Hopefully by now you can easily identify the three vital components of a boundary-setting conversation: the other person's behavior, the consequence, and your response. By clearly stating the behavior, consequence, and your planned response, you've set the stage for no surprises. The components in this order will generate the most clarity for the other person:

- *Behavior:* "When you choose to [state the troubling behavior],
- *Consequence:* [state how the behavior affects you].
- *Response:* The next time you choose to [behavior], I will [state your new response]."

Here are some examples of what it might sound like to put all three components together in a boundary-setting statement:

- "When you call me names, I feel humiliated and hurt. The next time you choose to call me a disrespectful name, I will leave the room."

- "When you raise your voice at me, I feel intimidated and unsafe. Going forward, the next time you raise your voice at me, I will go spend the rest of the evening with my friends Pat or Chris."

> BY CLEARLY STATING THE BEHAVIOR, CONSEQUENCE, AND YOUR PLANNED RESPONSE, YOU'VE SET THE STAGE FOR NO SURPRISES.

- "When you spend most of the weekend golfing and not helping me with the kids, I can't get to do some of the things I want to do. I'm exhausted by Sunday night, and it leaves me feeling angry and abandoned. The next time you choose to be absent for most of the weekend, I'll take the kids to my parents and spend the weekend there."

- "When you interrupt me during team meetings, it undermines my leadership, makes it hard for me to move us through my presentation, and leaves me feeling hurt and frustrated. The next time you interrupt me during a presentation, I will stop you immediately, ask you to hold any comments until the end, and request that you be more considerate in the future."

- "When you ask me to give you money for gas, it creates financial strain on me and I feel taken advantage of. Moving forward, when you ask me for money, I'm going to say no."

5. ANTICIPATE REACTIONS AND RISKS

No one enjoys it when you stop carrying the negative consequences of their bad behavior. The person you're setting the boundary with has something to gain by getting you to continue with the status quo, your over-accepting and under-protecting. When you set a boundary, the other person realizes that they will now be the sole owner of their own adverse consequences. It's never easy to accept that we generate negative consequences, let alone face the prospect of retaking possession of them.

Setting a boundary with someone places increased distance between you and them. This can leave the other person feeling rejected or abandoned, even if this wasn't your intention. This distance almost always provokes fear, which is often expressed as anger by those experiencing your new limitations. So expect a protest.

Resistance to boundary setting is an almost universal experience. It would be wonderful if, after engaging in a boundary-setting conversation, the other person praised your wise, reasonable decision and stopped the troubling behavior, forever and for all eternity. Unfortunately, that's just not something that usually happens, at least not initially.

In all my years of setting boundaries in my own life—and coaching others to set boundaries in theirs—I have never heard of someone's initial reaction being, "Thank you so much! I'm so glad you had the courage to set a boundary with me. My behavior has been so annoying. I now see the error of my ways. How could I have missed this? From now on, I will keep the consequences of my bad behavior to myself."

Don't let the fact that others will protest stop you from setting a necessary boundary and protecting yourself. Let the likelihood of resistance motivate you to prepare before setting a boundary, so you won't be surprised or caught off guard *when*—not *if*—they react poorly.

A poor initial reaction is perfectly normal. You can hope that over time, the other person will see the error of their ways, develop insight, and be convicted to change their behavior so you'll no longer need to protect yourself from their adverse consequences. But this isn't the reason we set boundaries. We've said this a lot, but let's drive the point home. Boundaries are defense, not offense. We set them to protect ourselves, not to prompt change in other people.

So be prepared. Enter the boundary-setting process with full expectation that you'll receive resistance. In general, the bigger the boundary, the bigger the negative reaction. People desperately want to maintain the status quo, especially if it benefits them. Typically, they will turn up the heat in the hope of avoiding your boundary. If you fail to anticipate some of the hurtful or manipulative things they may say or do, you're more likely to be provoked by their reaction, and either slip back into your old pattern of relating or make matters worse by reacting poorly.

Anticipating statements of resistance will help you remain calm, kind, and courageous when they happen. Here is a list of common responses people use to try to get someone to back down from setting a boundary and return to the status quo:

- "How could you do this to me?"
- "You used to be so kind, but now you're just self-centered and mean."
- "Don't you ever think of anyone besides yourself?"
- "If you really loved me, you would not do this."
- "If you really loved our kids, you would not do this."
- "And you call yourself a Christian?"
- "What kind of mother [or father, friend, etc.] would do that?"
- "Why can't you just accept me as I am?"
- "After all I have done for you, this is what I get?"
- "Just once, it would be great if you took my hurts and needs into consideration."
- "Where does it say that you have to be selfish and set boundaries?"
- "I can't do anything right in your eyes."
- "Maybe I should set a boundary on *you* for all the crap you do wrong!"
- "So that's it? Just like that, you're throwing us away?"

- "This is just your excuse to not do your work."
- "You've always been too sensitive."
- "This is just your excuse to abandon me."
- "I guess you don't value my friendship as much as I value yours."
- "This is just your excuse to avoid having a hard conversation."
- "What you're doing is not biblical!"
- "Here we go again, with you only thinking about yourself."
- "Here we go again, with you blaming me for all your problems."
- "I get that we need to make some changes, but the way you're going about it is all wrong."
- "Is this really what they teach you at your church?"
- "So this is what 'unconditional love' looks like?"
- "Is this what we get for all those counseling dollars we're spending?"

THE COST OF WAITING TOO LONG

One reason that a boundary-setting conversation is often so difficult is because we wait too long to have it. We avoid having the conversation until late in the game, rather than when the issue or behavior is new and less problematic. Now the issue has grown in its scope and scale, and the stakes have grown large and painful.

When the other person reacts poorly to your boundary-setting conversation, remember that up to this point, you've probably been over-accepting their undesired behavior. And your silence may have communicated that everything was fine.

If this is your situation, you have some culpability in having co-created the painful impasse both of you now face. Own that you have been part of the problem, and that you changing the status quo may feel like a bait-and-switch to the other person. Be patient with their negative response. But hold firm on your boundary decision.

Risks

If you have been dangerously over-accepting in a relationship, you may find yourself at risk of, or are experiencing, some form of harm or abuse. Or you may sense a relationship heading this way if you don't get out. Abuse comes in many forms: emotional, spiritual, verbal, physical, and sexual. If you sense it's time to set boundaries with someone you fear might react in a threatening or aggressive way, it's imperative that you seek help from a licensed therapist and establish a robust and safe support system before moving forward.

If you're currently in a relationship that has a history of risk of physical harm to you, I implore you to take action today. If you sense you might be in immediate danger, call the police. If you're not in immediate danger but fear you might be at risk of harm, then call your local or the national domestic violence hotline and get professional advice right away. Don't take risks with your safety. Err on the side of caution before you have any boundary-setting conversations with someone who may be dangerous.

AT RISK OF PHYSICAL HARM?

In immediate danger?
Call 911.

Not in immediate danger?
Contact the National Domestic Violence Hotline:
1–800-799-7233 | www.thehotline.org
Don't face this alone! Create a detailed safety plan.

PLANNING YOUR BOUNDARY-SETTING CONVERSATION

Craft and Practice Your Boundary-Setting Statement

Before reaching out to the person you want to set boundaries with, take time to prepare for your conversation by crafting and then practicing your boundary-setting statement. This helps ensure you've done all you can to help the conversation go as well as possible.

Using the three vital components we discussed earlier—behavior, consequences, and your planned response moving forward—write out what you want to say. It might take you several attempts to hone your comments into one or two concise sentences, but your effort will prepare you to have a helpful, productive conversation.

FORMULA:
BOUNDARY-SETTING STATEMENT

- When you choose to *[behavior]*, then *[consequence: how it affects you]*.
- Next time you choose to *[behavior]*, I will *[response: what you will do]*.

Remember this simple formula (see box above) and use it to phrase the three components of your boundary-setting statement into your own words. Once you feel confident about the clarity of your statement, practice saying it out loud until the words feel natural to you. Speaking the words aloud, to yourself or to someone from your support structure who has agreed to help you prepare for this conversation, may sound like a step you can forgo, but I urge you not to skip it. Not only will practicing your statement out loud help calm your nerves as you enter the conversation, something empowering happens when you hear yourself speak these words: you'll likely feel proud of the decision you've reached, and your courage will grow as you rest in the certainty that this boundary is necessary for the relationship to improve.

Plan the Setting and Logistics

The second step in planning your conversation is to decide the setting and logistics that will best help the conversation go well.

Think through the location, including which room in your house or whose office, what time of day, and what date on the calendar. If you have children, plan for a time when they're in bed, at school, or out of your care.

If you'll be speaking with someone who tends to power up on you, choose a location that is your "turf," or is at least neutral ground. For example, don't choose the other person's office if they are your boss, because you'd then begin the conversation in a one-down position of power. Choose a setting that will feel safe to both of you. The best scenario you can imagine is your plan A. In addition to plan A, think of some plan B and plan C scenarios in case the other person isn't available for your plan A setting, time, or day.

Once you're confident you've done a thorough job in preparing to set a boundary, it's time to have the boundary-setting conversation.

NINE

During the Conversation

WHERE WE'RE HEADED:

The work you must do *during* the
boundary-setting conversation:

1. Be kind
2. Be courageous
3. Be clear

You've prepared for a boundary-setting conversation by planning a boundary-setting statement with three vital components:

behavior + consequence = response

You've invested time practicing what you'll say, and you've come up with plans A, B, and C for when and where the conversation could take place. Now it's time to have the conversation.

The conversation will last longer than your one- or two-sentence boundary-setting statement, as both of you exchange thoughts and feelings. For the conversation to go well, three important characteristics must define your words and posture: you should be kind, courageous, and clear.

1. BE KIND

By the time you get to the point where you're ready to set a boundary with someone, being kind isn't necessarily your highest motivator. Often you're feeling frustrated and hurt in the relationship, and you just want the pain to stop. If you've waited so long before setting boundaries that you're feeling hopeless or desperate, then the last thing on your mind is preserving the relationship, let alone being kind.

Some people equate kindness with weakness. They fear being kind makes them look soft and risks their needs being ignored by the other person. If you're worried about this, don't be discouraged. You can set boundaries with kindness and still stay fully committed to rejecting the status quo and embracing a new pattern of relating, moving forward.

Kindness matters. The goal of a boundary-setting conversation isn't to make the other person pay for their past behavior; it's simply to increase protection for yourself at a level appropriate to your situation, while being as accepting as possible toward the other person. Remember, boundaries are about defense, not offense. Status quo isn't kind, either for you or for the other person. It's actually unkind to allow someone to continue engaging in hurtful behavior and say nothing. By finding that ideal balance between protecting and accepting, you retain the highest likelihood of bringing health, healing, and safety to the relationship.

If your pattern of over-accepting in a relationship has left you with pent-up resentment, it's only natural to want to lash out at the person who's been hurting you for far too long. It takes discipline to resist the temptation to hurt the other person or seek some sort of justice. For your boundary-setting conversation to be effective, you must be kind. By measuring each word against how our List 1 people would respond, we can get to the other side of the process without regretting that we somehow made things worse.

What does kindness look like when it comes to setting a

boundary? The following are four ways we can be kind during a boundary-setting conversation. The first two, starting soft and avoiding criticism, minimize the chances of us provoking or offending the other person early on in the conversation. The last two, reassuring and validating, help minimize the other person's fear of abandonment or being misunderstood.

Use a Soft Start

Solid research demonstrates that in the vast majority of cases, the trajectory established in the first few seconds of an intense conversation will determine the outcome of that conversation. This remains true even when the conversation gets off on a rough start and then one party attempts to repair or soften the tone. Marriage and relationship expert John Gottman states:

> Research shows that if your discussion begins with a harsh startup, it will inevitably end on a negative note, even if there are a lot of attempts to "make nice" in between. Statistics tell the story: 96 percent of the time you can predict the outcome of a conversation based on the first three minutes of the fifteen-minute interaction![1]

The trouble lies in the fact that the brain's limbic system, specifically the amygdala, can recognize a potential threat and initiate a fight-or-flight response in us *before* the rational part of the brain, the neocortex, has time to recognize the words another person is saying. Once your limbic system sounds the alarm and releases its reflexive, defensive cascade of neurochemicals, your rational, relational neocortex can get overridden, making it less available to help get the conversation back on track.

The first few minutes of your conversation matter greatly. So begin the conversation when you're calm and not feeling triggered, angry, or contemptuous. If your primary emotion is anger, you likely have more personal inner work to do before you're ready to have this conversation. When you have adequately right-sized your gap and realize you need to place protective distance between yourself and the other person by setting a boundary, the emotions you feel are often substantial sadness and sorrow, not anger.

Because the first few seconds of your conversation are so important, consider scripting out your first couple of lines; then practice delivering them in a calm and kind manner. Say them in front of a mirror so you can see your facial expressions, or in front of a trusted, safe friend who could offer feedback.

If the conversation is at high risk for going poorly, or if you're someone who is uncomfortable having these types of conversations, you might find it useful to memorize your first few lines or to bring a written copy and read from it to avoid a harsh start-up.

Don't Criticize

When setting a boundary, your focus is on defense. This isn't the time to argue, blame, or shame the other person for past choices or behaviors. This conversation is about giving notice of your future responses to troubling behavior, not about winning a past argument or getting the other person to see the error of their ways. If you allow the conversation to devolve into an argument, you've lost any chance for a kind, courageous, and clear conversation. Save any necessary debate for later conversations.

When you've reached the point where you need to set a boundary, you've most likely been hurt by the other person's behavior, and the temptation to zing them during this conversation can be irresistible. Remember, when you describe consequences that you're no longer going to carry for the other person, you're not critiquing them; you're simply stating a fact. Don't let passive-aggressive language slip into your statements.

Below are some examples of well-crafted, helpful boundary phrases, and some unhelpful ones that allow hurt to leak out in the form of criticism:

Unhelpful: Because of your selfish pattern of spending money . . .

Helpful: Because your pattern of spending money beyond our budget has put an extra burden on me . . .

Unhelpful: As a result of your refusal to grow up and act like an adult . . .

Helpful: As a result of your choice to spend so many evenings out with friends instead of at home with me and the kids . . .

Unhelpful: Since you continue to be irresponsible and reckless . . .

Helpful: Since you continue to drink and then drive our car . . .

Unhelpful: Since you continue to be dishonoring . . .

Helpful: Since you continue to arrive late . . .

Unhelpful: Since you're too lazy to get off the couch and look for a job . . .

Helpful: Since you have chosen not to contribute financially to our expenses . . .

Remember, setting a boundary will likely provoke resistance, defensiveness, and perhaps shame in the other person. Shame sabotages their capacity to feel genuine conviction, because it prompts them either to defend themselves or to isolate. Therefore it's all the more important not to trigger their shame unnecessarily with a carelessly phrased boundary statement or a conversation poisoned with criticism.

Ideally, when faced with a future of owning the consequences of their own behavior, the other person will respond with conviction. True conviction will move them toward repentance, changed behavior, and relational repair. While you have no control over how they will respond to your boundaries, you give them the best chance of responding well if you avoid criticism.

Sincerely Reassure the Other Person

When someone is setting boundaries with me, my instinctive reaction is to feel like I'm in danger. The limbic system in my brain takes over, and my rational/relational neocortex is pushed off-line. When I am in this state, I'm so preoccupied with how I can get myself out of danger that I can't hear the specifics of what the other person is trying to tell me.

And I'm not alone. This response to perceived danger is quite common, universal, in fact, which is why it's so important to reassure the other person of our commitment to them and to the relationship when we're setting boundaries. Unless a relationship is so toxic that you're cutting the person out of your life completely, take steps to reassure the person that you value them and the relationship before you introduce the boundary. Offering reassurance helps prevent their limbic systems from throwing them into fight-or-flight mode, and helps their neocortex to stay engaged so they can hear and remember the conversation.

Let the other person know the boundary isn't intended to hurt or reject them; it's just intended to protect yourself. Since most people react to boundaries with a fear

> UNLESS A RELATIONSHIP IS SO TOXIC THAT YOU'RE CUTTING THE PERSON OUT OF YOUR LIFE COMPLETELY, TAKE STEPS TO REASSURE THE PERSON THAT YOU VALUE THEM AND THE RELATIONSHIP BEFORE YOU INTRODUCE THE BOUNDARY.

of rejection or abandonment, your reassurance can minimize the amount of avoidable fear and discomfort they'll feel. Don't water down or minimize the real issue to soften the blow; instead, offer sincere reassurance of both your commitment to the relationship *and* your commitment to protecting yourself from the consequences of undesired behavior on their part.

The key word here is *sincere*. Don't say anything you don't really believe. A boundary conversation that is kind, courageous, and clear is rooted in honesty and truth. Prepare your thoughts ahead of time so you can offer whatever reassurance you can, with integrity.

Here are a few examples of opening sentences that provide reassurance:

- "I want to have a hard conversation with you, but first I want to reassure you that my long-term goal is for our relationship to succeed."
- "You're an important person in my life, and I want our friendship to grow stronger. But for that to happen, I need to set a boundary in one area of how we relate to each other."
- "I want to talk about our current pattern of relating. I'm not trying to pull away from you. In fact, my desire is to create an environment that will allow our relationship to survive and heal. But to do so, I need to set a boundary."
- "First, let me reassure you that you're my daughter and I love you unconditionally, no matter what, and I always will. This conversation might be difficult, but I'm hoping a new way of responding to you will allow us both to grow and be better able to relate."

If the other person has perpetuated trauma or abuse against you, don't promise a future relationship. Seek guidance from a licensed counselor who can help you navigate a boundary conversation with a harmful person. But in most cases, it's possible, and extremely helpful, to reassure the other person that your goal isn't to end the relationship but to improve it by protecting yourself.

Own and Validate What You Can

When someone has been making choices that result in negative consequences that you've been carrying, it's hard to remember or even recognize that you, too, have contributed to the problems in the relationship. None of us are innocent. It takes two to create a relationship that isn't working, even if the other person's contributions are glaringly more significant than yours.

It's important to be honest and humble when setting a boundary. You might be tempted to avoid mentioning your contributions to a relational gap, because you don't want to give the other person ammunition to start a debate or make the problem your fault. Here is where the work that you did earlier to right-size the gap will pay off. Owning your part will help the other person see that your new way of responding to disappointment in the relationship will be rooted in fairness and humility. Here's what owning and validating your contribution might sound like:

- "I recognize that I've been part of the problem in perpetuating this unhealthy pattern between us. I have not been clear with you about the impact of your overspending all these years. That's not fair, and I'm sorry. So it's probably very hard for you when I tell you that, starting today, I need the pattern to change by both of us committing to live on a budget."
- "I realize that I've made matters worse with my pattern of using passive and destructive ways of resisting your drinking in the past, which probably adds to your current sense of abandonment. I'm truly sorry, and I'll do my best to improve in this area."
- "I recognize that I've nagged and criticized you a lot over the last year. This certainly couldn't have added motivation for you to spend more time with me and the kids. I'm sorry."

- "I confess that, instead of being mature and direct with you, I have managed my disappointment by diving into my work and my outside friendships. This has left you feeling like I don't care for you. I want to correct that pattern of avoidance."
- "I realize that I have my own problems that contribute to our relational issues, and that I've hurt you. So going forward, I'm going to see a counselor weekly about my anger, and commit to limiting myself to only one drink when I'm out with friends."

If the rhythm of over-accepting has been ongoing for a long season, it may be best to admit that you lacked the courage, know-how, or wisdom to give voice to your concerns sooner, and that, in time, this lapse contributed to your unhealthy pattern. Had you responded earlier, the boundary might not have been necessary, or the conversation would have been less painful.

As tempting as it may be in these situations, don't distort your apology into a passive-aggressive way to zing the other person by saying something like, "I am sorry I put up with your terrible behavior for so long." These thinly veiled criticisms never help.

A Story of the Late Employee

A few years ago, I needed to set a boundary with a direct report who habitually came late to meetings. This person was a new and valued part of our team, and I let this problem go on for far too long before speaking up, which was quite unfair to her. Before I set a boundary about her punctuality issue, I had to own my part in the problem.

Here's a snapshot of how I attempted to own my part before setting the boundary and describing new expectations moving forward:

I need to begin by apologizing for not giving voice to this issue last year when I first noticed that you would sometimes arrive late to our meetings. I was afraid of embarrassing you, because you were new. But I now realize that by not saying anything, I actually communicated that being late is no big deal. So now that I'm addressing it, it must feel like a bait-and-switch to you, like I'm changing the rules of the game. I apologize. I should have been clear sooner. But moving forward, here's what I expect . . .

We then discussed a new set of expectations for punctuality, and because I was able to own the parts that were truly and sincerely my fault, I think it minimized the amount of embarrassment and hurt this valued staff member felt.

When you look back on your boundary-setting conversation, you'll want to have as few regrets as possible. Regrets usually come in the form of having been too harsh, too unprepared, or too unclear. I've never known anyone who regretted being too kind, unless they were confusing kindness with weakness. Kindness is never weak. When someone tells me, "I was too nice when I set the boundaries," usually, upon reflection, they realize they failed to pair their kindness with appropriate levels of strength. The problem wasn't too much kindness; the problem was too little courage.

2. BE COURAGEOUS

For most of us, being kind is the easy part. The hard part, especially for sensitive, empathetic people who tend to be pleasers, is keeping courage in play.

As mentioned previously, there are several reasons why we feel fear or insecurity when setting a boundary:

- Most people react to having boundaries set with feelings of fear, loss, shame, or hurt, and may react with anger.
- Status quo is comfortable, and it's tempting to take the easy way out rather than stand firm.
- Even if only in small ways, you, like all of us, contribute to

the problem in relationships; your lack of complete innocence makes you more likely to second-guess yourself and your decisions when it comes to setting a boundary.

In a relationship that needs renovation, a number of underground factors will tempt you to settle for the status quo. Returning to the familiar way of relating with this person will seem very appealing when the protecting process gets tough. The old arrangement has its benefits, even if it was merely the financial stability or relational predictability. And even if the downside of the status quo exceeds the upside, the temptation to backpedal or soften your position can be strong. How do you choose courage over comfort?

Imagine you're having a boundary-setting conversation. You used a soft start and a kind tone. You reassured the other person as much as you could with integrity and sincerity, but what you feared might happen actually happens: the person responds strongly to your words, perhaps with anger, or they erupt in tears, panic, or accusations of betrayal.

If you haven't prepared for this kind of resistance, you might get flustered, triggered, or angry in return. You might be tempted to abort the mission altogether, lightening up on your boundary and settling for an easier compromise. Losing courage when the conversation gets hard only reinforces the arguments or aggressions of the other person, making your efforts to protect yourself all the more difficult in the future. If you settle for an easier conversation now, you can expect to see the same unhealthy relational patterns reappear, more galvanized than ever before.

Be attentive to old patterns that have kept you carrying the burden of the other person's consequences. Remind yourself of the reasons this conversation must happen, and the conclusions you've come to beforehand. Keep in mind:

- You've right-sized the gap so you know what's *really* going on (reality), and you're clear on what you *really* want (desires).

- The status quo is no longer acceptable. The relationship needs some renovation.
- You're no longer willing to carry the consequences of the other person's troubling behavior or choices.
- Setting a boundary is the wise and mature thing to do.
- You're not seeking revenge or justice.
- You're not trying to change or control the other person.
- You've identified where you've contributed to the problem and have owned and validated your contributions.
- You've reassured the person where you could, with sincerity.

Now it's time to add courage to your kindness and manage your relational disappointment with the poise and maturity of a confident, wise adult.

The presence of courage does not replace kindness; rather, it augments kindness. Courage does not mean aggression or anger. Your facial expressions, tone of voice, and words must remain as warm and reassuring as possible, without softening or abandoning the boundary or swinging toward aggression. Courage is rooted in kind confidence, not aggression.

COURAGE IS ROOTED IN KIND CONFIDENCE, NOT AGGRESSION.

This isn't a time to reenter the dialogue from scratch. Simply execute your plan and follow through. Tell the whole truth, and transfer the negative consequences back to their rightful owner.

3. BE CLEAR

As we discussed in chapter 8, one of the most common reasons for boundary failure is a lack of clarity during the boundary-setting conversation. We can maximize clarity by being attentive to both the quality and quantity of our words.

The person with whom you're setting a boundary will likely not agree with your assessment of the relationship and probably won't like the decision you're making to set a boundary. But, by choosing simple, direct words, you can be sure that they will at least understand what to expect in the new, post-boundary reality. After this conversation, they will be clear on why you're setting a boundary and what you plan to do the next time their undesired behavior sends consequences your way.

To provide this kind of clarity, your words must be specific. Going forward, you want all parties involved to be clear on how you plan to *specifically* respond to which *specific* situation. Use concrete words.

Not specific: If you drink too much, I'll leave.

Specific: If you have more than two drinks when we're on a date, I will immediately call Uber and get a ride home.

Not specific: If you're mean, I won't tolerate it.

Specific: If you call me names or criticize me in front of the staff, I will stand up and leave the room.

Not specific: If you spend too much, I'll stop you.

Specific: If you spend beyond our monthly budget, I'll split our finances into two accounts, and you'll be solely responsible for paying your half of the bills from now on.

Make It a Short and Stand-Alone Conversation

When we drown our boundary-setting statement in a sea of words and topics, we sabotage clarity. To maximize clarity, keep your conversation short and to the point. It should be a focused, stand-alone discussion with only one central topic: your planned response to the other person's troubling behavior moving forward. Period.

Tacking on the boundary-setting conversation to the end of a different, lengthy discussion muddies the conversation with extra words and topics. If you've been rehashing the same old disputes or arguing about the troublesome behavior with the other person, don't announce your new boundary in that moment. The timing will make your boundary seem like a rash decision or a punitive response, rather than a thought-out, purposeful decision. This increases the likelihood that the other person will react harshly or dismiss your boundary altogether.

By planning for and engaging in a concise, stand-alone boundary conversation, the other person will see you as calm, rational, and determined. Use as few words as necessary to give clarity to the other person with the three vital components of your boundary-setting statement.

Your three-part boundary-setting statement should be simple, clear, and to the point. This is not the time to tack on additional things you don't like about the other person, nor is it time to vent and get things off your chest. Adding extra words or new topics distracts from the specific boundary you're setting for a specific situation. It also raises the risk of the other person feeling attacked, which makes it hard for them to hear your boundary.

Resist the temptation to use inflammatory phrases like the following in your conversation:

- "I am sick and tired of . . ."
- "I'm not going to take it anymore."
- "You always do this to me."
- "My family [or friend, etc.] agrees with me."
- "How could you do this to me?"
- "I have lost respect for you."

Your goal isn't to win a war. It's to create a future environment that protects you from carrying the negative consequences of the other person's choices, so that your relationship is more likely to heal and succeed.

BEHAVIOR (WHEN YOU . . .)	CONSEQUENCE	RESPONSE (I WILL . . .)
drink too much at a party,	you get loud and inappropriate.	drive myself home. You can call a taxi.
slander or gossip about others,	you disrespect me and the people you're gossiping about.	leave the room immediately.
spend money beyond our budget,	we are not able to put money into the savings to protect our family's financial future.	open my own bank account and separate our bills and credit cards.
don't honor our rule of not smoking or drinking in the house,	the house smells like cigarettes, and it sets a bad example for your younger brothers.	ask you to move out of our basement and find your own place.
spend your money on video games instead of paying your half of the rent,	I must either pay for both of us or be delinquent.	ask you to move out and find a new roommate.
schedule an event on a Sunday morning,	we miss church.	not attend the event with you, unless we've discussed it at least a week in advance and made adjustments accordingly.
get angry and then drive fast and aggressively,	you put my safety at risk.	insist that you stop the car and let me out. I won't get in the car with you again until you've seen a therapist about your anger.
are not ready to leave for the airport on time,	you put me at risk of missing our flight.	leave for the airport at the time we agreed on, and you can call a taxi when you're ready.
give me a work project after 4:00 p.m.,	I can't finish in time to make my 5:30 p.m. train.	work hard on the project until 5:15 p.m., then finish the next morning.

BEHAVIOR (WHEN YOU...)	CONSEQUENCE	RESPONSE (I WILL...)
have contact with your former affair partner,	it re-breaks trust with me.	move out and begin to rebuild my life without you.
belittle me in public,	you disrespect and embarrass me in front of others.	call a taxi and go spend the night at my dad's place.
don't look for a job but still ask to borrow money,	you have no way to pay me back.	say no to your request from now on.
don't complete your part of the project on time,	the rest of the team must pick up your slack.	not help you finish your part, and I won't cover for you if the boss asks why we're late.

NOW WHAT?

YOUR GOAL ISN'T TO WIN A WAR. IT'S TO CREATE A FUTURE ENVIRONMENT THAT PROTECTS YOU FROM CARRYING THE NEGATIVE CONSEQUENCES OF THE OTHER PERSON'S CHOICES, SO THAT YOUR RELATIONSHIP IS MORE LIKELY TO HEAL AND SUCCEED.

You've invested time in preparing a clear and concise boundary-setting script for your conversation. You've delivered it in a kind, courageous, and clear fashion. And in doing so, you're changing the long-established dance in your relationship by telling the other person that you will no longer carry the consequences of their unacceptable behavior.

Boundary-setting statements usually prompt energetic responses from the people you're setting boundaries with. Is your role in setting a boundary complete once the conversation is over? Far from it. In many ways, the more important elements of setting boundaries are still to come.

TEN

AFTER THE CONVERSATION

WHERE WE'RE HEADED:

The work you must do *after* the boundary-setting conversation:

1. Stay connected to safe people
2. Don't react to their reaction
3. Empathize with, but don't assume ownership of, their feelings
4. Don't be swayed by your own negative internal voices—stay the course

Congratulations! You had the conversation. You set a boundary. Your work is done, right? Nope. The boundary-setting conversation isn't the finish line. It is actually the starting line.

Before you take a deep sigh of relief and enjoy the benefits of balanced levels of accepting and protecting in the relationship, recognize that your work isn't complete. With rare exception, entering into a respectful, grown-up, boundary-setting conversation is a deviation from the norm. It upsets the status quo.

While there are countless variations to the relational patterns that existed in the weeks and years that led up to the boundary-setting conversation, both parties had specific roles they've been accustomed to playing. One may have been the avoider and the other the pursuer. One may have been aggressive and the other passive-aggressive. One may have played the role of abuser and the other the role of victim. One may have been the needy one and the other the tireless helper. Whatever the combo, the dance had two willing participants who've become skilled in their unique dance steps.

The bottom line is this: you and the other person have perfected a dance that will be difficult for *both* of you to stop. When you cease doing your part in the old dance, your dance partner will feel incredibly uncomfortable; they will often do everything in their power to regain the status quo and get you to resume the steps that keep the same old dance going. And, most likely, they know exactly how to push your buttons to get you back into the dance.

This is why your post-conversation work is so important. You've done the hard work of setting a new course; now it's time to do the work of staying on that course.

Here are four tasks to help you make continued progress in maintaining the new, healthy balance of protecting and accepting in your relationship.

> YOU'VE DONE THE HARD WORK OF SETTING A NEW COURSE; NOW IT'S TIME TO DO THE WORK OF STAYING ON THAT COURSE.

1. STAY CONNECTED TO SAFE PEOPLE

One of your pre-conversation tasks from chapter 8 was to seek a safe, stable support system of people to come alongside you throughout the boundary-setting journey. Their involvement is no doubt valuable as you prepare to set a boundary with someone. But the need for these people will be even more important after the boundary is set.

One mistake many of us make after setting a boundary is to let self-doubt take root. As soon as the conversation is over, we begin asking ourselves if we made too big a deal out of the situation, if we said the right things, or if the boundary was too harsh. Your tribe of safe people can help you stay the course, remind you of why you set the boundary in the first place, and support you in maintaining optimal levels of accepting and protecting in the relationship moving forward.

Who are the safe people in your post-boundary life? Sometimes the safe pre-boundary friends fade afterward, either because they're uncomfortable with the new status quo, or they're not willing to stand with you against the negative reaction of the other person. Other times, people who weren't part of your original support system show up to help you after the boundary is set; they're kind, courageous, and present in meaningful and helpful ways. Anticipate that your group of safe people will experience some shifts. That's normal.

If the boundary you set results in a significant change in your life, your tribe of safe people should include a therapist and a same-gender close friend (as mentioned in chapter 8). These two individuals know you, understand your story, and will be able to point out when you start to veer off course on your journey toward better relationships. Your tribe can help you stay out of either the "too harsh" or the "too soft" ditch as you interact with the other person.

2. DON'T REACT TO THEIR REACTION

The other person will almost certainly resist your boundary because no one likes to have a boundary set against them. Your task is to not be surprised by their reaction. Don't react in an unproductive way when the other person resists your boundary.

This is where your hard work in chapter 8, anticipating the other person's reaction, will really pay off. By anticipating the most likely negative reaction, you can prepare *your* reaction to *their* reaction. Prepare your new dance step so that when the other person reflexively reacts to your boundary, you won't reflexively return to your old, unproductive dance step.

Without this anticipation, the boundary-reaction-reaction pattern can look something like this:

- You set a boundary.
- The other person reacts strongly, showing anger, aggression, tears, and such.
- You second-guess your decision—back down, compromise, or surrender your boundary and your voice—returning to the status quo.

Dang. All that hard work for nothing. Instead of reverting to the same old dance, be prepared to stay strong and not back down, even if the other person reacts more strongly than you anticipated.

Or, perhaps your familiar pattern looks more like this:

- You make efforts at setting a boundary.
- The other person reacts critically: they remind you of how you have failed in the relationship, restarting the all-too-familiar argument about how the problems are really due to *your* choices and behavior, not theirs.
- You feel unheard, frustrated, and attacked, so you react with your own version of blaming, criticizing, and defensiveness, returning to the familiar logjam argument that leaves you both feeling hopeless and victimized.

In this case, the other person has some incentive to turn the tables with a comment like, "You're the one who's hurtful in this relationship! I should be setting a boundary with *you!*"

In the moments, hours, and days that follow the boundary-setting conversation, don't get seduced into your old pattern of relating. If you get emotionally triggered by the other person's reaction to your new boundary, you're more likely to react by returning to the status quo in the relationship. The key is to catch yourself as soon as you get triggered, before you have a chance to react in unhelpful ways.

Are you clear on what it feels like when you start to get triggered emotionally? In the heat of battle, do you notice when your emotional escalation begins? If not, this will be important work to conduct with your therapist and friends. Develop a plan to help you remain calm and stay the course, before you get triggered and lose access to the rational parts of your brain during future interactions with this person.

3. EMPATHIZE WITH, BUT DON'T ASSUME OWNERSHIP OF, THEIR FEELINGS

For people who are naturally wired toward over-accepting, showing empathy for how someone else feels comes easily. But setting boundaries can create substantial inner tension. It's tempting to slip back into comfortable roles of rescuer or enabler when past voices whisper, *Can't you just get along? Why did you make such a big deal?* or *Just be nice*, as if carrying the consequences of someone else's bad behavior is somehow nice. How do we stay truly nice without slipping into the dark side of over-accepting, enabling, or codependency? It takes discipline and practice to show genuine empathy for the discomfort our boundary has created for someone else, *without* taking on their discomfort as our own.

> IT TAKES DISCIPLINE AND PRACTICE TO SHOW GENUINE EMPATHY FOR THE DISCOMFORT OUR BOUNDARY HAS CREATED FOR SOMEONE ELSE, *WITHOUT* TAKING ON THEIR DISCOMFORT AS OUR OWN.

If your habit has been to rescue the other person from the consequences of their own behavior and assume responsibility for their problems, then you might feel pressure to accept responsibility for any fear or hurt they feel when you set your boundary. You will be tempted to own their discomfort by soft-pedaling your boundary or removing your newfound limits altogether.

Be aware of some common tools the other person may use, either intentionally or unwittingly, to convince you to lighten your boundary and resume ownership of consequences that belong to them.

Watch for Aggressive Attempts to Transfer Responsibility Back to You

On the aggressive side, the other person might use phrases designed to make you feel as if you're being self-centered or making a big mistake, such as:

- "This boundary is just your excuse to be selfish and get your way."
- "If you weren't in so much denial about your own problems, you wouldn't be blaming everything on me."
- "I thought we raised you better. How could you be so disrespectful to your own parents?"
- "And I thought you were a Christian! Doesn't the Bible say to be kind?"

This strategy is unnerving, because it taps into some of the very fears you had to overcome before you set the boundary in the first place. The other person may try to make you feel guilty, or even threaten you with further consequences.

When someone lobs these types of aggressive remarks your way, remind yourself that you've already spent many careful hours right-sizing the gap and preparing for this conversation, and your safe, stable support system affirmed your strategy. Recognize the other person's aggressive remarks for what they are: attempts to transfer ownership of their consequences back to you. Don't give in to these threats. Stay the course by expressing empathy for how they must be feeling, but then affirm your decision and restate your boundary.

Aggressive attempts to transfer responsibility can be fairly easy to spot because of their high levels of amperage and volatility. But they're no less damaging to relationships than their passive counterparts.

Watch for Passive Attempts to Transfer Responsibility Back to You

In passive attempts to transfer responsibility back onto you, the other person works quietly and diligently to convince you to pick up their consequences. They hope you'll resume carrying the consequences of their bad behavior because you feel sorry for them. In this tactic, the other person doesn't resist the boundary per se; rather, they express deep sadness and fear about what will become of them in this new arrangement. How will they survive? How will they possibly get along without your support?

The passive style of transferring ownership of their consequences might sound like the following:

- "I guess that's it then. You're done with me. I always feared I would grow old alone."
- "How pathetic is that? I'm the kind of guy that even his own parents can't stand to be with."
- "Maybe I'm just not made to survive in this world."
- "I guess I should have never chosen this career in the first place. I just dreamed too big."

This tactic, though more passive, creates significant tension inside you if you tend to over-accept in relationships. You're a nice person. You love to help and serve others. So it's really hard to pass over an opportunity to soothe the ache of someone, particularly if that someone is a family member or someone you care about. Their strategy of making you feel sorry for them hooks something that is truly lovely about you. But if you don't recognize these types of comments as passive attempts to transfer ownership, then what's beautiful about you will become distorted, and the result will be further harm to the relationship.

In those moments after you've set a boundary and you're feeling empathy for the other person's sadness, fear, or anger, be attuned to their reactions, whether aggressive or passive. Choose your response carefully, and don't let their attempts to transfer responsibility back onto you lead you toward old patterns. Offer empathy for how your boundary must make them feel, but only to the degree that you can do so sincerely. Then renew your commitment to both the relationship and your new boundary, maintaining ideal levels of accepting and protecting moving forward.

Here are some examples of statements that express both empathy and a commitment to the boundary:

- "I'm sad that you're so unhappy with this boundary. While I'm not willing to reconsider that decision, I'm very interested in us discovering how we can have kind and productive interactions in this new season."
- "This seems hard for you, and I'm sorry for that. I'm hopeful for the day when we're better able to manage this issue with less strict and detailed boundaries. But for today, I need this space."
- "I want to be able to hear and understand you when you express yourself. Going forward, is there a way for us to discuss this without you expressing your anger this way?"
- "It sounds like it's hard for you to accept this boundary until we have more dialogue about my contribution to our problems. That makes sense. I'm not able to postpone the boundary at this time, but I'm committed to continuing to explore and understand my mistakes leading up to this point."

- "I feel sad that you have anxiety about how you'll manage this new arrangement. I hope you can find additional support through counseling or your other friendships."

4. Don't Be Swayed by Your Own Negative Internal Voices—Stay the Course

If you've shifted course from over-accepting to a more protect-ing stance in a relationship, it's common to experience some self-doubt. Even after you've done the work of identifying the unproductive voices of self-deception (accuse others and excuse our-selves; minimize the problem and rationalize our contribution), you might be left with a lingering negative internal voice—your own inner critic.

Most people have moments of fear and doubt. We're haunted by internal questions that include the word *really* like this:

- *What if the things she said about me really are true?*
- *Am I really a horrible son?*
- *Am I really a disrespectful employee?*
- *Have I really failed my kids?*
- *Am I really expecting too much?*
- *Am I really a bad parent?*
- *Have I really abandoned my responsibilities?*
- *Is all this really worth it?*
- *Am I really that selfish?*
- *Am I really taking the easy way out?*
- *Am I really that hard to get along with?*

These thoughts likely have roots in our families of origin or the unhealthy and hurtful parts of past relationships, and at some level, there might be tiny bits of truth. We all miss the mark at times. We let

WE ALL MISS THE MARK AT TIMES. WE LET OTHERS DOWN, THINK ONLY OF OURSELVES, OR ARE HARD TO GET ALONG WITH. BUT DON'T LET THESE NUGGETS OF TRUTH GROW INTO MOUNTAINS OF DOUBT. others down, think only of ourselves, or are hard to get along with. But don't let these nuggets of truth grow into mountains of doubt. Own the parts that are (or were) true, but stand firm, knowing that in this relationship, or in this season, your boundary is justified, wise, and firm.

In the meantime, you have done the work. You have renovated your relationship. Now it's time to follow through. Maintain this new way of relating, stay protected from consequences that don't belong to you, and honor your boundary.

You can do it.

Stay the course.

PART IV

FROM START TO FINISH

WHERE WE'RE HEADED:

- *Renovate Your Relationships Summary Sheet*
- Case Study: Brad and Tony

From identifying and right-sizing a relational gap, to choosing an ideal strategy of accepting or protecting, to setting defensive boundaries in a way that improves the relationship, we've covered a lot of ground in the preceding ten chapters.

We all learn differently. Although reading about concepts in chapter format is essential, sometimes it helps to see how those concepts actually play out in conversations. What wording did people use? Where did they get hung up? What was the turning point?

In part IV, we walk through a real-life scenario (names and details have been changed to protect privacy) where all the concepts in this book play out in narrative form. This case study recounts a relational disappointment of my friend Brad. His story is a textbook example of someone navigating a significant relational gap by applying many of the skills you've learned in this book.

It's time to put the concepts in this book together, from start to finish. I invite you to be a fly on the wall, observing how Brad used boundary setting to renovate his relationship with his middle son, Tony.

The *Renovate Your Relationships Pathway* chart below is a summary of the entire process outlined in this book. As you read the story of Tony and Brad, you may want to refer to this sheet to track Brad's progress. It may provide helpful reminders for you as well, as you chart your own course.

You can download a printable version of this pathway from my website, https://www.ScottVaudrey.com/Resources.

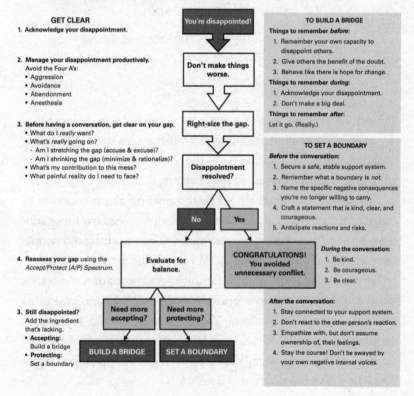

RENOVATE YOUR RELATIONSHIPS PATHWAY

GET CLEAR

1. Acknowledge your disappointment.

2. **Manage your disappointment productively.**
   Avoid the Four A's:
   • Aggression
   • Avoidance
   • Abandonment
   • Anesthesia

3. **Before having a conversation, get clear on your gap.**
   • What do I *really* want?
   • What's *really* going on?
     - Am I stretching the gap (accuse & excuse)?
     - Am I shrinking the gap (minimize & rationalize)?
   • What's my contribution to this mess?
   • What painful reality do I need to face?

4. Reassess your gap using the *Accept/Protect (A/P) Spectrum.*

3. Still disappointed?
   Add the ingredient that's lacking.
   • Accepting:
     Build a bridge
   • Protecting:
     Set a boundary

You're disappointed!

Don't make things worse.

Right-size the gap.

Disappointment resolved?

No / Yes

Evaluate for balance.

Need more accepting? / **Need more protecting?**

BUILD A BRIDGE / **SET A BOUNDARY**

CONGRATULATIONS!
You avoided unnecessary conflict.

TO BUILD A BRIDGE

Things to remember *before*:
1. Remember your own capacity to disappoint others.
2. Give others the benefit of the doubt.
3. Behave like there is hope for change.

Things to remember *during*:
1. Acknowledge your disappointment.
2. Don't make a big deal.

Things to remember *after*:
Let it go. (Really.)

TO SET A BOUNDARY

Before the conversation:
1. Secure a safe, stable support system.
2. Remember what a boundary is *not*.
3. Name the specific negative consequences you're no longer willing to carry.
4. Craft a statement that is kind, clear, and courageous.
5. Anticipate reactions and risks.

During the conversation:
1. Be kind.
2. Be courageous.
3. Be clear.

After the conversation:
1. Stay connected to your support system.
2. Don't react to the other person's reaction.
3. Empathize with, but don't assume ownership of, their feelings.
4. Stay the course! Don't be swayed by your own negative internal voices.

ELEVEN

CASE STUDY: BRAD AND TONY

It had been a few years since I had seen my old friend Brad. He was in Chicago for business and drove out to the suburbs one night to join us for dinner and catch up. After dinner, he opened up to me about his middle son, Tony, who was now twenty-eight.

Tony had always been a bright, winsome young man, but following a couple of big hits in his life, Brad was growing deeply concerned about him. Last year, Tony got laid off from his well-paying job in the city, and then his live-in girlfriend, Megan, whom he'd hoped to marry, broke up with him and moved out.

"He's been in a major funk ever since," Brad said. "At first his sadness seemed appropriate. He'd lost his girlfriend and his job, and he was stuck paying rent on this expensive downtown apartment all by himself. Barb [Brad's wife] and I really felt bad for him, so we invited him to move back home till he could get his feet under him again."

But since moving home, Tony hasn't made any effort to look for work or rebound relationally. He's reconnected with a group of old high school friends with minimum-wage jobs, and they sit in Brad's basement all day, playing video games and drinking beer. It seems Tony has become the proverbial "adult kid living in his parents' basement." Brad knew something had to change.

"It's been over a year now," he said. "Barb and I offered to pay for counseling, in case he's depressed, but he's not interested.

Confrontation isn't easy for me. I'm a bit of a people pleaser. But I knew I needed to have a hard conversation with my son, so a few months ago after dinner one night, I bolstered my courage and dove in."

Based on Brad's recounting, here's how Round One of their conversation went:

Brad: Hey Tony, can we talk about the future?

Tony: Depends. Your future or mine?

Brad: Yours, son. Seems like it's time for some new direction.

Tony: No thanks. Not interested in having that conversation.

Brad: Well, how long are you going to be content doing nothing with your life?!

Tony: What part of "no thanks" did you not understand, Dad?!

Brad: You sit on your butt all day playing video games with your loser friends, while I work to pay for it!

And with that, Tony left the dinner table and retreated to the basement, slamming the door behind him. The cold war had begun.

"I really blew it," Brad told me. "I flew off the handle. That's how it always goes with us. Tony can trigger me like no one else! My frustration just builds over time until the dam bursts. But what am I supposed to do?"

RIGHT-SIZING THE GAP

Desires: What Does Brad *Really* Want?

Brad felt deeply concerned about Tony's current way of living, but he wasn't sure what to do.

"What do you want, really?" I asked him.

"In a perfect world," he said, "I'd want Tony to be a hardworking, responsible adult who supports himself and doesn't abuse alcohol. And in my dream sequence, he'd probably be married and cranking out some grandkids for me by now."

Brad wisely recognized that, while it was fine to wish for his son to have a wife and kids, it wasn't reasonable of him to expect this. Brad's first task was to recognize that, despite his efforts, he can't control Tony or force any outcomes. The only thing under Brad's control was himself, and how he responded to his son.

"Okay, so of the things you can control," I asked, "what do *you* really want?"

With more focus to the question, Brad tried to filter through all the disappointing aspects of his current reality with Tony. "What I want most right now," he said, "is to change how we're relating. I am feeling so taken advantage of right now."

I introduced Brad to the concept of boundaries. "Setting a boundary," I said, "means keeping adverse consequences with their rightful owner."

"Exactly!" Brad said. "That's what I need. Barb and I are on the receiving end of Tony's bad choices. It's not fair. I want to shove those consequences right back in his lap."

Brad and I spent time talking about how to name those adverse consequences, figure out who owns what, and state what he really wants in specific terms. The conversation went something like this:

Brad: Okay, here's one consequence of Tony's choices I want to give back to him: I'm sick of worrying about him!

Me: Makes sense that you feel worried. But who is the rightful owner of your worry?

Brad: Uh, well, I guess I am. But it's Tony's fault!

Me: Tony has that much power over your emotions?

Brad: What? Don't you ever worry about your kids?

Me: Absolutely! But that's not their problem. I'm the owner of my own emotions, including worry. My kids aren't responsible for my worry, even if their choices or behaviors trouble me and tempt me to worry.

Brad: Okay, fine. I'll own my worry. But I'm also angry! I suppose I need to own my anger too?

Me: Yup.

Brad: Dang. But how about this, I'm sick of his laziness. He's super marketable in his field, but he won't even look for a job.

Me: Makes sense. Tell me more.

Brad: He sleeps in till ten or eleven every morning. I can't stand it.

Me: So, how are you carrying the consequences of Tony sleeping in?

Brad: I'm not sure. I mean, I'm not his alarm clock.

Me: So, if he started getting up every morning at 6:00 a.m., would that solve your frustration with his laziness?

Brad: No. He needs to get a job!

Me: So, if you went home today and found out that Tony had landed a decent job, you'd be satisfied?

Brad: Maybe. If he gave me some money toward groceries and paid his own bills! He's a grown man, but I still pay for everything like when he was a teenager. I pay for his cell phone, car insurance, gas, food, hot water, everything. I'm even paying for all the beer Tony and his buddies are suck-ing down! Barb and I are trying to save for retirement, and all those expenses really add up.

Me: Got it. So the adverse consequence of Tony not working is that he can't pay his bills, so you're paying those bills, right?

Brad: Yes. Those are the consequences I want to get rid of. I'm carrying his inability to pay his way in life.

Me: This is where setting a boundary could be helpful.

Brad: But we've already set boundaries with him over this issue. We've told him we would like him to get a job by the end of the month, but each month comes and goes and he still won't look for work.

Me: Telling him to get a job by the end of the month isn't setting a boundary. That's just being controlling. If the con-sequence you're carrying for him is that you're paying his bills, then one boundary you could set might be to stop pay-ing his bills.

Brad: But he can't pay his own bills without a job!

Me: Correct. But that's for Tony to figure out. Does this make sense?

Brad: Ahhh. Got it. I'm carrying the consequences of Tony's lack of job by paying his bills. So I can just stop?

Me: Sure. That is an option under your control. But, remember, you only set a boundary to protect yourself and not to pun-ish or control your son.

Brad: Hmm. I confess that part of me wants things to get pain-ful, so he'll grow up.

Me: That's a reasonable desire. But let's be clear, setting a boundary is only aimed at managing things under your control. So, one consequence is the amount of money you're shelling out. Anything else?

Brad: Yes. He's a slob. Our house is a constant mess because he never picks up after himself. Barb and I both hate having a messy house, so we're constantly cleaning up after him.

Me: So, the consequence you're owning for Tony's messiness is that you feel you must either live in a messy house or clean up messes that you did not create. Is that it?

Brad: Yes!

Me: Got it. Anything else?

Brad: Um, yes. The noise! He and his friends come and go at all hours of the night. Doors slam, and then the dog barks. Plus, they play their video games super loud. They wake us up, and it affects our sleep.

Me: So, currently, you're owning the consequences of Tony's late-night habits by losing sleep. What would be a reasonable time for you to expect to get to bed and not have your sleep disrupted?

Brad: Maybe 10:00 p.m.? I don't think that's too much to ask.

Me: All right. Anything else?

Brad: One more thing. Kevin! Tony's creepy friend. I hate that kid. He's a thief and a drug addict. He's no longer allowed in our house because he stole some tools from the garage. Tony should stop hanging out with him.

Me: Okay, but are you carrying any consequences of Tony hanging out with Kevin?

Brad: Well, he drinks too much when they're out together.

Me: So clearly Kevin isn't a good influence on Tony. But now that Kevin is no longer allowed in your house, it doesn't sound like their friendship is causing you to carry any new consequences that belong to him or Tony. You set a good boundary after the tools were stolen, but their continued friendship isn't really an issue from which you need to protect yourself with another boundary. Would you agree?

Brad: I guess so. This falls in the same category as my worry and my anger. I might be unhappy about him hanging out with Kevin, but I can't blame him for how I feel. My emotions aren't consequences he has forced on me.

Me: Exactly. Anything else?

Brad: Hmmm. Nope. Those are the biggies.

Me: So to summarize your answer to, What do I *really* want? these are the three consequences you want to hand back to Tony:

1. The financial drain of him living in your house without contributing.
2. Disrupted sleep after 10:00 p.m. when he and his friends come and go and play their video games loudly.
3. Messy house because he doesn't clean up after himself.

Does that about capture it?

Brad: Yes. That's a pretty thorough summary. There are other things I wish for him, for his own sake, like for him to find a fulfilling career, good friends, maybe a wife and kids. But in terms of consequences I want to hand back to him, that's about it.

Brad's struggle to focus on the consequences of which he's not the owner is a common one. It helps to remind ourselves that boundaries are defense. They cannot control someone else; they can only keep adverse consequences with their rightful owner. While it would be great if Tony were to stop spending his days playing video games and drinking beer, get a job, become an early riser, and find respectable friends, none of those outcomes are under Brad's control. Brad named three consequences of Tony's behavior that he no longer wants to carry because Tony is their rightful owner. Now that Brad has identified the issues over which he has control, he can respond to Tony's destructive behaviors.

Brad and I covered a lot of ground that night over dinner. But this was just the beginning of his journey. He knew himself well enough to know he wasn't just a victim of Tony's choices; he had played a role in contributing to their strained relationship as well. Back at home, he began paying visits to his therapist, Lou, to gain clarity on his contributions.

Reality: What's *Really* Going On?

To gain clarity on the strain in their relationship, Brad needed to find answers to the second question of right-sizing the gap: What's *really* going on? In their next counseling session, Lou spent some time educating Brad on the human tendency to distort reality through self-deception. Brad and I spoke later that night.

"I recognized quickly that I've been distorting reality for quite a while by downplaying these issues with Tony," he said. "I was making the gap seem smaller than it actually was, which helped me feel justified in not setting boundaries with him sooner."

Brad did a great job of describing his *shrinking style* of self-deception. During our dinner, he'd said things like, "At least Tony isn't doing drugs," and "This is just how millennials live," to minimize the problem. And he'd rationalized his lack of action with statements like, "What Tony needs from me is my unconditional love," and "There's no expiration date on being a dad, right? I can keep supporting him if I need to."

But since their recent blowup when he'd tried to talk with Tony about his future, Brad had switched strategies. Out of frustration, he'd begun using the *stretching style* of self-deception.

"I went from being all soft on Tony to making him into a villain who could do no right," Brad said. "I began thinking of his behavior as worse than it actually is, sort of exaggerating how hard he's making things for me and Barb."

To use the language of "right-sizing the gap," Brad was justifying his anger by *exaggerating* the size of the relational gap. I recalled comments he'd made over dinner that *accused* Tony ("He's just plain lazy and disrespectful!") and *excused* himself ("I've done all I can to help him, and this is the thanks I get?").

Another important truth that emerged during Brad's counseling sessions with Lou was this: Brad was embarrassed that his high-achieving son was currently underperforming. "It's painful when friends ask about the family," he admitted. "I don't want to tell them what's really going on with Tony, and I'm tempted to lie, or at least leave out much of the uncomfortable truth about how Tony's life is progressing."

"I am not proud of this . . . but I've always dreamed my son's success would make me feel proud—and look good in the community. I've had to come to terms with the fact that it's important to me to be viewed as a great and successful father, but those are *my* dreams, not Tony's."

His feelings made sense, and they explained some of the energy he had toward getting Tony to shape up. "I know my first priority should be to love and support my son," he added. "And I'm ashamed to admit that sometimes I care more about my own embarrassment than Tony's reality."

"What you're feeling sounds pretty normal," I told him. "But I'm glad you're naming it. Give yourself permission to be disappointed, and even a little embarrassed. But remember, only you, and not Tony, are the rightful owner of those feelings. Your embarrassment cannot be your motivation for wanting to set boundaries with your son. You're setting boundaries to protect yourself from the consequences of Tony's actions. This will allow you to work on your relationship with him, free of resentment."

Lou also helped Brad see how his failure to communicate clear expectations with Tony before he moved home had contributed to the problems. "If I'd had a conversation in the beginning, or if I'd expressed my concerns when things started bothering me in those first weeks," Brad recounted, "then the issues wouldn't have become so big before we talked about them, and we wouldn't be facing an established pattern of many months that will be hard to break."

Brad's passivity in those early days will definitely contribute to the level of discomfort Tony will experience when boundaries are finally set. I was impressed with Brad's level of ownership for how he'd contributed to the problem, and felt confident that he'd enter the boundary-setting conversation with Tony with sincere humility and softness toward his son.

Lou helped Brad get to this point of humbleness and ownership for his contributions by posing some of the helpful questions from *Crucial Conversations*,[1] which we discussed in chapter 6:

- Why would a decent and reasonable person behave like this person is behaving?
- What is my contribution to this mess?
- What painful reality do I need to face?

Their conversation went something like this:

Lou: So, Brad, what do you think is your contribution to the conflict you're having with your son?

Brad: I think I've been too loving, too nice. I just waited too long to put my foot down.

Lou: Hmm. Being "loving" and "nice" sound like good things. I'm not sure it's a problem to be loving and nice. Is there a different word that might be more accurate to describe your conduct with Tony?

Brad: I'm not sure. How do I figure that out?

Lou: Well, as you look back over the last year or so, and you sense you've contributed in some way to your relational problems, what's one word that really captures how you've behaved with Tony?

Brad: Oh boy. I haven't been too nice. I've been too chicken! I've been afraid to say anything even when I knew I should. I've been a coward!

Lou: Coward is a pretty harsh word, though I suspect that it may be closer to the truth than being too loving or nice. Describe what you mean by "coward."

Brad: I should have been direct and honest much sooner. Instead, until I finally blew up at dinner the other night, I've acted like everything was fine on the outside, but inside I let my disappointment in Tony leak out in passive-aggressive ways. I've let resentment build up.

Lou: Got it. So let me check my understanding. You remained silent and kept supporting Tony financially, cleaning up after him, and being subjected to the late-night noise from him and his friends, all to avoid conflict and try to please him. And now you're filled with frustration to the point of contempt. Does that sound right?

Brad: Yeah, but I don't like the sound of that. It sounds weak.

Lou: Another word comes to mind. Codependent.

Brad: I'm not codependent!

Lou: I'm not sure the label is all that important. But would you agree that your fear of facing Tony's anger, rejection, or disappointment has held you captive? That it resulted in you not managing your disappointment in a timely and courageous way?

Brad: Yes! Definitely.

Lou: Got it. Have there been times when you covered for Tony so he would escape the natural consequences of his actions?

Brad: Sure. What parent wouldn't do that?

Lou: Is it safe to say there are times that, in lieu of being courageous and straightforward, you sometimes try to get Tony to change his behavior or choices by controlling or manipulating him?

Brad: Sometimes . . .

Lou: All right. So, forget the word *codependent* for a minute. Whatever word you use to describe your pattern, you seem open to the reality that you have a tendency to control and manipulate Tony. True?

Brad: Sure.

Lou: The next question is, "What painful reality am I afraid to name?"

Brad: Oh man. I'm codependent.

As Brad continued to make progress in therapy, the cold war with his son escalated. Brad became increasingly resentful and contemptuous as Tony continued honing his video game skills in the basement. In the process of working toward a clear picture of what's really going on, Brad journaled about the first of the three helpful questions: Why would a decent and reasonable person behave like Tony is behaving right now?

Following is an excerpt he emailed me from his journal entry that day:

> Well, for starters, Tony is young. When I was his age, if my parents had offered me free room and board and agreed to pay all my bills, I may well have taken them up on that offer myself. Who wouldn't want a season of not having to take responsibility and just enjoy life, especially after a couple of painful setbacks?
>
> Also, Tony's heart is broken. He is lonely, and I bet he's scared. He thought he'd marry Megan, and now maybe he's wondering, *What if I end up alone?* Maybe he's content to live in the basement because he's a bit depressed. If I were in his situation, I'd probably be depressed too. Maybe instead of being lazy and a taker, Tony is just sad and doesn't know what to do.

"After I journaled, I was able to give Tony the benefit of the doubt," Brad told me over the phone that night. "I began to feel increased empathy and sadness for my son. Don't get me wrong. I'm still hurt and angry. But after writing out all those thoughts, the predominant emotion I felt was sadness."

"And when you reach the point of sadness rather than anger or other secondary emotions," I said, "you know you've gotten closer to the root issues. I'm so sorry for your sadness, Brad. And I'm also very impressed by how you're navigating all this."

We talked about the concepts of accepting and protecting. I explained how, in each of our relationships, when we find the ideal balance of accepting and protecting, it runs smoothly, and we minimize the gap.

"Sometimes when a relationship gets out of balance," I said, "we need to increase the amount of accepting or protecting we've been applying in order for it to remain healthy."

"With Tony, I've been way off balance, with too much accepting," he concluded. "I need more protecting."

"I think you're right," I said.

Brad had arrived at a healthy place and reached the following conclusions:

- There is a gap in his relationship with Tony.
- The status quo with Tony is no longer acceptable. The relationship needed some renovation.
- He has been over-accepting of the situation, and it's time to adjust his response by adding increased levels of protecting.
- It's time to set a boundary.

And with that, Brad decided to start from scratch on the task of setting a boundary with Tony. I emailed him the *Renovate Your Relationships Pathway* chart to help him prepare his boundary-setting conversation and avoid another blowup like the one they had several weeks back.

"But even as you prepare to set boundaries using the pathway," I told him, "the process of managing your relational disappointment and setting those boundaries will still be hard. And when it gets hard, you'll be tempted to revert back to the familiar patterns that were comfortable, even when you know those patterns made things worse. It's human nature."

Brad was motivated not to slip back to his codependent patterns with Tony. He had good clarity on why he needed to add more protecting to their relationship. He wanted to:

- Provide unconditional love and reasonable levels of support to his hurting son.
- Parent and guide his son as appropriate.
- Defend himself and Barb from carrying consequences that belong to Tony.
- Stop distorting the gap by minimizing, rationalizing, accusing, and excusing.
- Stop being a codependent contributor to the problem.

BRAD'S TO-DO LIST *BEFORE* THE BOUNDARY-SETTING CONVERSATION WITH TONY

1. Secure a safe, stable support system.
2. Remember what a boundary is *not*.
3. Get clear on the adverse consequences you're transferring back to their rightful owner.
4. Decide on specific boundaries that are clear, kind, and courageous.
5. Anticipate reactions and risks.

Let's follow Brad as he tackles the five "before the boundary-setting conversation" tasks.

1. Secure a Safe, Stable Support System

Brad and Barb have a strong marriage, and they supported one another in this season. But the support of one person isn't enough. Brad was feeling desperate, and he needed honest feedback from wise people who knew him well, friends who would be both kind and courageous when he asked for counsel, and quick to help him spot his own contributions to the problem. He reached out to two trusted male friends.

"Don't let me just rant about Tony," he told them. "Redirect me if I'm just complaining or whining. I'll need your insights."

Brad continued seeing his counselor, Lou, and talking to me by phone for emotional support. He also began attending a twelve-step recovery group to understand his tendency toward being codependent.

2. Remember What a Boundary Is *Not*

When Brad took an honest look at the motives behind his responses to Tony thus far, he realized that he had been motivated more by trying to change his son and repair his own image as a dad than by protecting himself from Tony's consequences. Specifically, Brad was worried about Tony and the prospect of him wasting his life, or worse, making a big mistake while hanging out with the wrong crowd.

There is nothing wrong with a parent wanting to influence their child in positive ways. It would be good and reasonable for Brad to try to offer counsel and support for his son during this hard time; Tony clearly needed benevolent parental direction. But Brad needed to distinguish between parental direction and setting boundaries.

In his healthy desire to influence Tony, Brad had been *bargaining* with his son: "Tony, to encourage you in your journey toward finding a new job, I'll continue paying your car insurance as long as you secure one new job interview each week."

These types of enticements may be reasonable strategies for providing parental guidance and support, but they're not boundaries. Brad knew he was beginning to do the work of true boundary setting when his thoughts shifted from offense to defense. He wasn't trying to get Tony to behave a certain way or get his life in order; he was simply keeping the adverse consequences of Tony's way of life with their rightful owner.

3. Get Clear on the Adverse Consequences You're Transferring Back to Their Rightful Owner

In my first conversation with Brad, he sifted through and separated his desires and expectations for Tony from the *negative consequences* he and Barb were carrying from Tony's choices. Brad decided there were three specific consequences he wanted to return to Tony, the rightful owner: the financial drain of Tony living in their house without contributing; Brad's disrupted sleep after 10:00 p.m.; and a messy house because Tony doesn't clean up after himself.

Let's examine each consequence more closely.

Financial Drain

Currently Tony is taking up the entire basement without making any financial contribution. Therefore, Brad is funding his room, board, utilities, phone, video games, food, and beer budget. This has created a financial burden on Brad, who is trying to save for retirement. In addition, he'd hoped to celebrate his and Barb's thirty-fifth anniversary by taking her on a cruise through the Panama Canal, but now he's wondering if they can afford such a trip.

Disrupted Sleep

Brad and Barb had been enjoying their empty-nest season for several years before Tony moved back home. Having the entire house to themselves—with the corresponding peace, quiet, and privacy after raising three active children—had been a blessing. They'd been happy to surrender their empty nest to help Tony, but now that he has established himself as a somewhat permanent occupant of the basement, the steady influx of strangers coming and going at all hours means noise, lack of privacy, and music until well after midnight, even on weeknights.

Brad and Barb have a pattern of going to bed no later than 10:00 p.m., which allows them to keep their schedule of rising at 6:00 a.m. each morning. The current arrangement is adversely impacting Brad's sleep, which has ripple effects on his early morning routine, energy level, and work performance.

Messy House

Brad and Barb both value a well-maintained home, so it's unsettling to have the entire basement in utter disarray. They feel embarrassed when they need to go into the basement with a friend or service-person. Moreover, Tony's messiness has found its way upstairs. When they awoke in the morning, they would find a kitchen full of dirty dishes and a living room filled with Tony's clutter.

4. Decide on Specific Boundaries That Are Clear, Kind, and Courageous

Long before our initial conversation, Brad thought he'd set a boundary with Tony. But he'd made the common mistake of being vague and unspecific:

Brad: Tony, I think we need to negotiate about how our financial arrangement is going.

Tony: Okay. What do you mean?

Brad: I'm concerned that you don't have a job, and your mother and I are paying all the bills.

Tony: But that's why you invited me to move home, to help me out. What do you want from me?

Brad: I want you to start looking for a job or else I'm going to rethink how much support we can offer.

Tony: Okay, got it. Will do.

Brad thought he'd set a boundary. In his mind, *he* felt clear on what he expected from Tony and what would happen if Tony didn't comply. But he failed the clarity test in three areas:

1. *The* consequences *he was carrying:* Brad hadn't told Tony about the consequences that he was carrying as a result of Tony's

choices. This omission left Tony assuming Brad was just resorting to his unhelpful pattern of trying to change and control. Brad should have mentioned that the continued financial support meant he couldn't adequately save for retirement or take that thirty-fifth anniversary cruise with his wife.

2. *The specific* expectation *he was handing Tony:* "Start looking for a job" could mean many things. How often? What kind of job? Was there a deadline for him to find a job?

3. *The* boundary *he was setting:* "Rethink how much support we can offer" doesn't describe what will look different in the future. Tony had no way of knowing what to expect moving forward.

Fast-forward eight weeks, and Tony still didn't have a job, leaving Brad seething internally and harboring significant resentment toward his son. But Tony was still oblivious because Brad had been unclear.

Finally, one afternoon, when they crossed paths in the kitchen, Brad's resentment leaked.

Brad: I've had enough of you taking advantage of me!

Tony: What? What are you talking about?

Brad: I told you two months ago to get a job or else I'll stop paying your way for everything!

Tony: Are you kidding me? You told me to *start looking* for a job, and I've been doing that.

Brad: Oh really?! And what exactly have you done to find work?

Tony: I've been online several times this week looking for job openings!

Brad: *Online?* Well, that's certainly hitting the pavement. What a *hard worker* you are!

The conversation devolved into hurtful name-calling in both directions, with Tony, yet again, storming out of the kitchen and retreating back into the basement.

This scene demonstrates why clarity is so important. Brad and Tony had completely different interpretations of their earlier conversation. Each time Brad broached the topic with Tony, his desire to not inflame or offend his son resulted in a vagueness that, in the end, only inflamed and offended his son. Without clarity on the consequences Brad and Barb were carrying, what the problem behavior was, or what Tony's response might look like, Brad had not only failed to set a boundary but had set the stage for continued mismatched expectations and arguments.

"I learned the hard way about the cost of not thinking through specific consequences and boundaries *prior* to having a boundary-setting discussion with Tony," Brad told me over the phone. "If I have any hope of creating a sustainable and healing arrangement with my son, I need to get crystal clear on the details of the boundary!"

The goal of clarity is not to reach mutual agreement on the boundary, but to reach mutual understanding. It's human nature to resist having boundaries placed on us, so it's rare that two parties will see boundaries eye-to-eye. Tony's resistance to Brad's boundaries is perfectly normal. Brad needs to ensure that the descriptions of the specific problem *behaviors*, the resulting *consequences*, and the summary of how Brad intends to respond from now on (the *boundary*) are so crystal clear that anyone listening would understand what to expect in the future.

THE GOAL OF CLARITY IS NOT TO REACH MUTUAL AGREEMENT ON THE BOUNDARY, BUT TO REACH MUTUAL UNDERSTANDING.

After our last phone call, Brad began preparing to set some boundaries with Tony, using the three-part formula described in chapter 8: Behavior + Consequence = Response.

- *Behavior:* the troubling choices or behaviors of the other person that affect you
- *Consequence:* the negative consequence you've been carrying
- *Response:* how you will respond to the behavior from now on

Below is a summary of Brad's notes as he prepared for the conversation with his son.

Behavior

1. Not making any financial contribution to the family's expenses
2. Noise and disruption late into the night
3. Messiness

Consequences

1. *We're carrying 100 percent of your financial burden:* "This has created some budget strain for your mother and me. We aren't saving for retirement, and we're now unable to take the Panama cruise."
2. *Our sleep is disrupted after 10:00 p.m.:* "Your mother and I aren't getting the sleep we need, and it's adversely impacting our 6:00 a.m. morning routine. Because of this, we're tired during the day."
3. *Stress because of a messy house:* "We can't relax when the house is a mess, and we don't want to spend our time cleaning up after you."

Response

1. *Financial drain:* "Currently we provide your rent, food, utilities, cell phone, and car insurance. Starting May 1, we expect you to contribute $500 a month toward your expenses. By August 1, we expect you to contribute $1,000 a month. During this time, we'll continue to pay for cable, utilities, your cell phone, and all food, but we will no longer pay for your alcohol

or video games. If, by May 1, you're unable or unwilling to pay the $500 a month, then we'll stop paying for your cell phone, cable, and car insurance. If, by August 1, you're not able or willing to pay $1,000 a month, we'll have to ask you to move out."

2. *Disrupted sleep:* "Starting immediately, after 10:00 p.m., you must keep the volume of your games, movies, and conversation downstairs low enough that we don't hear them in our bedroom. We'll give you one grace slipup, but after that if the noise level wakes us up after 10:00 p.m., then going forward your guests must leave the house by 10:00 p.m., and no new guests can arrive after that time. If this boundary is violated, we'll ask you to move out and give you one month to find a new place to live."

3. *Messy house:* "Starting immediately, we expect the entire basement to be picked up, vacuumed, dusted, and the downstairs bathroom fully cleaned once a week. In addition, we expect that you put your dirty dishes only in the dishwasher, not in the sink or on the table, and that you keep your belongings in the basement, not left about in the living room. If the messy house becomes a problem on three more occasions (we'll give you two grace slipups), we'll ask you to move out and give you one month to find a new place to live."

These three boundaries are clear. While Tony may not agree on the necessity of these boundaries, he and his parents will have little trouble agreeing on whether these criteria have been met.

Notice what isn't said here: Brad didn't say he expects Tony to get a job, stop playing video games, stop drinking beer, or improve his choice of friends. While these are all reasonable desires Brad and Barb have for their son, they're not directly affected by the consequences against which they need to defend themselves. These three boundaries simply keep the consequences of Tony's choices with Tony.

5. Anticipate Reactions and Risks

Brad predicted that Tony wouldn't respond well to having boundaries placed on him, at least not initially. When planning his boundary-setting conversation, he knew he had to be realistic in anticipating how Tony might react. He didn't want to be caught by surprise like he had been with their two previous conversations, in which Tony stormed out and retreated to the basement.

Brad took plenty of time to think through the likely scenarios that would follow the boundary-setting discussion. He discussed this with his wife, a few close friends, and his counselor. Here are some of the possible unpleasant reactions he anticipated and planned for:

- *Tony might react with anger and say hurtful things:* Like most parent-child relationships, Tony really knows how to push Brad's buttons. Brad is particularly vulnerable when Tony accuses him of being controlling, which has been a sore spot between them. Tony has sometimes used this "trump card" to get Brad to either give in or explode.
- *Tony may choose not to pay the rent and end up homeless:* Although this possibility horrified Brad and Barb, by anticipating the worst-case scenarios ahead of time, they were able to discuss the implications of these boundaries and come to terms with them. They knew something needed to change and felt the likelihood of their son becoming homeless was small, but real. They agreed to move forward, understanding that this extreme outcome would be Tony's choice, and they cannot control him any longer.
- *Tony may move in with one of his less-desirable friends:* This possibility also horrified Brad and Barb, knowing these friends would be a bad influence on Tony's progress toward responsible adulthood. But Tony was a grown-up, and they recognized they should not try to control his decisions. They also felt hopeful that the bright, loving boy they had always known

Tony to be would eventually resurface, and he will begin making better choices.

- *Tony may threaten to move out and disown his parents:* Again, a terrifying thought, but not likely to happen. Still, it was a better option than contributing to their son's downfall by enabling his current lifestyle.

- *Tony may try to move in with relatives or family friends, or he might ask to borrow money from them:* This would heighten the awkwardness and embarrassment Brad and Barb already felt about Tony's situation. "But our pride can't be the motivator for us to lessen our boundaries," Barb reminded Brad. "We're the ones who need to own our embarrassment, not Tony."

Brad called me the day before his planned boundary-setting conversation with Tony. He'd prepared himself for the scenarios above. "And I'm praying for a kind, courageous, and clear conversation," he said. "I'll be heartbroken if Tony chooses a response that puts some relational distance between us, even for the short term. But the status quo will ultimately be more harmful to us all. It's time to do something different."

"Proud of you," I told him. "Are you emotionally prepared for the conversation to get uncomfortable? Because it probably will."

"I'm determined to be kind, clear, and courageous, even though it goes against my pattern of being too loving and nice," Brad said, laughing. "But I've learned a lot about my weak spots. If Tony reacts badly, I'll remind myself that it's probably scary for Tony to have these boundaries set. I'll be empathetic, because I really do feel for the guy. And I love him so much."

Brad spent time focusing on his deep love for his son, his desire for Tony to succeed, and his sadness over their current relational gap. He hoped his tender feelings toward Tony would be reflected in his tone of voice and facial expression during the conversation. And wanting to use a *soft start-up*, he carefully crafted and wrote out the specific phrases he'd use to open their conversation.

Brad and Barb asked Tony to talk after dinner. They both wanted to be present for the conversation to show a united front, but they decided that Brad would do most of the talking. Being clear on the specifics of their desires, the consequences, and their responses, he entered their meeting with sadness rather than anger. And if Tony responded poorly, he was prepared to stay strong, with Barb's support, without reacting harshly in turn. Brad was ready.

BRAD'S TO-DO LIST *DURING* THE BOUNDARY-SETTING CONVERSATION WITH TONY

1. Be kind
   - Use a soft start-up
   - Don't criticize
   - Sincerely reassure the other person
   - Own and validate what you can
2. Be courageous
3. Be clear
   - Use specific words
   - Make it a stand-alone conversation

Tony agreed to talk after dinner on a Sunday, a night when no one had evening plans, so the conversation would not be rushed.

Remembering that boundaries are put in place to save and heal a relationship, not to hurt the other person, seek justice, or score a victory, Brad began his boundary dialogue in a kind, calm, and warm tone. Here's a recap of their conversation. Notice that Brad's opening comments use a *soft start-up*, providing appropriate *reassurance* and *validating* how the other person feels.

Brad: Hey son, there's been a fair amount of tension between us lately, and I know I created a lot of that tension by reacting so harshly during that hard conversation we had after dinner a few weeks back. I want to begin by apologizing. I am really sorry about that.

Tony: Thanks, Dad. That's fine.

Brad: I want us to have a strong, adult relationship, one that survives hard times like this. So, with your permission, I want to take another stab at that discussion.

Tony: Okay . . .

Brad: I don't believe that our current living arrangement is an ideal or sustainable system, so I'm hoping we can discuss it and come out the other side with more trust and respect for each other as a result.

Tony: Oh, boy, here we go. Another lecture coming my way.

Brad: These conversations seem hard for you. They're hard for me too. And I need to take some responsibility here. I've made two big mistakes in how I've talked with you about this stuff.

First, I've been tentative and a bit unsure of how to proceed, and given my people-pleasing tendencies, I've stuffed some of my disappointments about our current situation and have been too afraid to speak my mind. I've waited far too long to have this conversation, which means we've now developed some less-than-ideal patterns that I want to address.

Second, I've let my frustration leak out at you in hurtful ways, like in our last conversation when I yelled at you. No excuses. You didn't deserve that. And I'm sorry. I hope you can forgive me.

Tony: Sure, Dad. Neither of us put our best foot forward that night.

Brad: It makes sense that you'd be leery about having more conversations about this stuff, because our previous ones have not gone well.

Tony: Yeah, it isn't exactly my favorite way to spend an evening.

Brad: Tony, I want to do a better job of walking with you and supporting you as you rebuild your life after a really tough season. I want to be more honest and timely in coming to you about how I'm feeling.

Tony: Thanks . . . I think.

Brad: Here comes the hard part of the conversation. Your mom and I feel we need to renegotiate some of the specifics of our living arrangement with you, okay?

Tony tensed up. He saw where this was headed and didn't like what he saw.

Tony: That's just super. I knew it. I knew it'd eventually come to this.

Brad: Son, we're hoping you can hear us with openness. We want you to understand things from our perspective.

Tony: Fine . . . go ahead.

Brad: Well, the current arrangement is having adverse consequences on your mom and me in three different areas. It's added extra pressure on us, and it's become too uncomfortable for your mother and me to ignore. So I'd like for us to discuss some new arrangements.

Tony: (sigh) Here we go again. What, do you want me out?

Brad: That's not what I'm saying, Tony. Your mother and I are great with you living with us while you're figuring things out. But to ensure a mutually rewarding, sustainable plan, we need to address these three issues: finances, noise levels late at night, and cleanliness.

Tony: And what if I don't agree? What if I don't address your three issues to your *controlling* satisfaction?

Brad: Well, I really hope that it doesn't come to that. And we're trying really hard not to control you, but simply to keep these adverse consequences in your lap, rather than in ours. Could you hear us out?

Tony: Fine.

Brad: Why don't we work through it now and see how it goes, all right?

Tony: No! What if I don't want to hear your plan? What if I don't agree with your new "rules"? Then what?! Are you going to just kick me out?!

Brad: Well, that would be very sad for us. And, yes, in the worst-case scenario, in the event that your decisions continue to adversely impact your mother and me to the degree they are currently, we would have to ask you to live elsewhere.

Notice that when Tony turned up the heat by using the hot-button word *controlling* in his response, Brad didn't take the bait. Instead, anticipating Tony's resistance and fear, he remained calm and didn't become defensive. Impressive. But when Tony's first volley didn't provoke or intimidate his dad, he raised the stakes.

Tony: Are you kidding me? You would throw your own son out onto the street?! You'd kick a man when he's down?! I can't believe what I'm hearing!

Brad: That's certainly not at all what we want. Our desire is to create and maintain an environment that will allow you to live at home until you choose to move out and get your own place. And also to maintain harmony in the house until then.

Tony: You mean you want to create *your* version of harmony.

Brad: Yep. That's right. The impact of some of your current patterns of living are uncomfortable for us, and we're hoping to address them so we can coexist in a manner that honors all of us. What we're suggesting is really quite reasonable. Why don't you hear me out before you jump to conclusions?

Tony: Fine, go ahead. Let the controlling begin!

Up to this point, Brad had done very well. When Tony tried to distract or provoke, he kept gently bringing the conversation back to the topic of setting a boundary. Knowing how important the wording of a boundary-setting statement is, Brad had written out exactly what he wanted to say. He opened his journal to read from his notes.

Tony: Seriously?! You've rehearsed what you want to say? What is this, some kind of reality TV show? Why don't you just tell me what you want to say?

Brad: I've blown it too many times with you when I try to wing it, son.

Tony: You got that right.

Brad: I know this looks sort of canned, but it really matters to me that I communicate well, so I wrote notes, and I'd like to use them, all right?

Tony: Fine.

Brad: Okay, so here are the adverse consequences from your current choices that are too uncomfortable for your mother and me to continue carrying:

1. We're carrying 100 percent of your financial burden, which has created some budget strain for us.
2. You and your friends disrupt our sleep after 10:00 p.m., and we aren't getting the amount of sleep we need.
3. You leave the house messy. The basement's a mess, you don't clean up in the kitchen, and you leave your stuff all over the living room. It's hard for us to relax when the house is a mess.

We would like to generate a plan that returns the responsibility and consequences of these choices back to you. Perhaps we can take them one at a time? Would that be okay?

Tony: No! This is BS!

Tony stood up to leave, but Brad remained calm.

Brad: I understand this is hard, son. Please stay with me. I want us to work together on solving this. It's an important and necessary discussion if you want to continue living with us. We love you and want to be here for you.

Tony hesitated, then sat back down, his arms crossed, clearly angry.

Tony: Fine. Go ahead.

Brad: All right. Thanks. Let's start with the finances. Your mother and I keep to a budget and spend our money carefully. Our current situation of supporting you is proving to be more of a financial drain than we can continue for the long term. Your auto and health insurance alone are costing us hundreds each month. We feel it's time that you help off-set at least some of the expenses of living here.

Tony: It's a little hard to contribute to the pot when I don't even have a job!

Brad: Yep, I understand that. If you need help brainstorming ways to find a job, we'd be happy to help with that part. But going forward, starting in seven weeks, on May 1, we expect you to contribute $500 a month for room, board, insurance, and expenses. We'll continue to pay for food, utilities, and your cell phone. You pay for your own enter-tainment, including alcohol.

Tony: Unbelievable! And exactly where am I going to get $500 by May 1? Rob a bank? Sell drugs, maybe?

Brad: I'm pretty sure you're capable of finding a more productive way to solve this problem than that. And, as I mentioned, we're happy to help brainstorm some ideas. But the problem is ultimately yours to solve.

Tony slumped in his chair but remained quiet.

Brad: Let's move on to the second issue, which is easier to deal with. Disrupted sleep. Your mother and I are both early ris-ers, and we really depend on our sleep. We usually head to bed by 9:00 p.m., and we'd like to be asleep no later than 10:00 p.m., because we get up at six in the morning. You and your friends play games and watch movies in the basement into the wee hours of the morning, and the noise wakes us up most nights.

So, going forward, we would like the entire house, includ-ing the basement, to be quiet enough after 10:00 p.m. that we do not hear noise in our bedroom. No loud coming and going after that, and no blaring movies or games in the basement.

Tony: But what if I'm having a party? You seriously want a party to be over by 10:00 p.m.? Even on weekends?!

Brad: If you're having a party or some special event, let's talk. We'll be reasonable, I promise. But for the vast majority of nights, quiet after 10:00 p.m. Seem fair enough?

Tony: But what if I can't keep my friends from making noise?

Brad: Great question. Part of this arrangement will require you to "train" your friends to some degree. You'll be responsible for setting the rules, not us. Here's what we're asking. The next time you or your friends wake us up after 10:00 p.m., we will let you know the next morning. If it happens again, then moving forward, we'll expect your friends to be out of the house by 10:00 p.m.

Tony: You have got to be kidding! I'm almost twenty-nine years old, and you want to give me a curfew?!

Brad: Oh, no. That's not what this is. We don't care how late you stay up, or how late you come home. We just don't want to be woken up unless there's an emergency. So we're transferring the negative impact of the noise you and your friends make back to you. Ever since you moved home, your mom and I have been the only ones experiencing adverse consequences for your noise. Now we're letting you be the one to carry those consequences. If you choose to continue to make noise late at night, you will need to find some other place to make it. Our house will be closed to noise after 10:00 p.m.

Tony: Brother. That's just great. Anything else?

Brad: One more thing. This one won't surprise you, because you'll remember it from your childhood. It's the issue of a messy house. Your mom and I both like to live in a clean house. Maybe not spotless, but at least picked up, dishes put away, floors semi-clean, and so on. It's hard for either of us to relax in a room that's messy. We've not wanted to micromanage your space in the basement, but, no offense, it's pretty bad down there.

And you leave a trail behind you up here as well. Moving forward, we want you to keep the basement clean. We don't care how you keep your bedroom down there, or if you make your bed. But in the rec room, we want floors picked up, carpet vacuumed weekly, and the downstairs bathroom cleaned really well at least once a week.

Tony: And if I don't pass your white glove test, you'll throw me out?

Tony was calling his dad's bluff, using sarcastic words and exaggerating what Brad and Barb were asking of him. Would Brad fold?

Brad: I'd hope that it doesn't come to that, but, eventually, yes. Similar to the plan with the noise issue, we'll give you a couple free slipups. The first two times you fail to keep the basement or main living space in decent condition, including a weekly vacuum of the rec room and a scrub of the downstairs bathroom, we'll bring it to your attention. If it happens more than twice, we'll ask you to live elsewhere and give you a month to find a new place. Whether you end up needing to move out is completely up to you.

Tony: Really?! What kind of parent tosses their kid out over a piece of popcorn on the carpet or a cereal bowl left in the sink? Seriously? What has gotten into you people?

Brad: We're sad if this makes you angry, Tony. But to be clear, we're not tossing you out. We're just placing reasonable expectations on you. You have full control over whether you choose to meet those expectations and stay. If you end up deciding to live somewhere else, we'll be sad. Except for the noise and cereal bowls, you're good company! But we're handing you back the consequence of your decisions. They're yours to own, not ours.

Tony: Sounds like you're just trying to dump me, like Megan did.

Brad heard the fear and pain underneath his son's protests.

Brad: Tony, we aren't dumping you, and we never will. We really want this boundary thing to go well, because we believe that, in the end, it will build our relationship and grow our trust in each other. It might not sound like it to you, but these three changes are actually our plan to make it possible for you to stay. Our goal is a healthier, grown-up relationship with you, not for you to move out.

Tony rubbed the palms of his hands against his eyes.

Tony: What a load of bull.

Brad: I'm sorry you're seeing it that way, son. But, just to summarize, here's what we're asking. Starting in seven weeks, on May 1, you pay $500 a month for room and board. We continue to pay for food, utilities, insurance, and your cell phone. You pay for your entertainment, which includes alcohol. Starting next week, the entire house, including the basement, is quiet each night after 10:00 p.m. And starting today, you clean up after yourself upstairs, and vacuum and clean your bathroom downstairs weekly. Would it help if I wrote this down for you?

Tony: That won't be necessary. Looks like it's time to pack up and find people who care about me.

And with that, Tony got up, stormed out of the room, and retreated to the basement, just like he'd done so many times before.

Brad and Barb looked at each other. The outcome of the conversation was so disappointing. But this time, Brad felt at peace. He and Barb were both heartbroken and a bit scared about what Tony would choose to do, but they didn't follow him downstairs.

Brad called me later that night.

"How'd it go?" I asked.

"Not great," he said, "but I think I stayed kind, clear, and courageous the whole time. Tony has no doubt what to expect moving forward. It got pretty dicey, and Tony pulled some of the same tricks that have always worked well in the past. But this time I didn't back down. Barb and I just let Tony storm out, the proud owner of his own consequences."

"Any regrets?"

"No regrets."

Brad's To-Do List *After* the Boundary-Setting Conversation with Tony

1. Stay connected to a safe, stable support system
2. Don't react to their reactions
3. Empathize with, but don't assume ownership of, their feelings
4. Don't be swayed by negative internal voices—stay the course

1. Stay Connected to a Safe, Stable Support System

During the first several weeks after the conversation, Brad made it a discipline to schedule regular times with his safe, stable community, seeking their input and staying in touch with his own emotions in the process. His rhythm of connecting with his inner circle looked like this:

- *Barb:* Brad and his wife had coffee together every morning at 6:00 a.m. and checked in with each other about how things were going.
- *Lou:* Brad and his counselor met weekly.
- *Small group:* Brad met with a small group of guys every other Tuesday. They were aware of his situation with Tony, and it helped him to report his progress and hear their encouragement.
- *Me:* Brad checked in with me by phone every other day in the first couple of weeks. Eventually, the pace slowed to once or twice a week.
- *Twelve-step group:* Brad continued to attend his support group for codependents during the tense months after the conversation.

This rhythm of maintaining access to a support system ensured that Brad would get regular feedback in maintaining good boundaries with Tony, all the while taking steps to build a bridge toward his son. At times when he felt frustrated with Tony's whining and self-pity, he had a safe place to vent his over-protecting thoughts: "Sometimes I wish he would just move out!"; or, when his confidence or courage sagged, he had a safe place to vent his over-accepting thoughts: "Sometimes I just want to give up on this whole boundary thing and let Tony do whatever the heck he wants." On both sides of the spectrum, his support system gave him the luxury of a wise and safe counsel, and people to hear him out, validate his frustrations, and urge him to stay mindful of the long-term goal: a mature, mutually trusting and growing relationship with his son.

2. Don't React to Their Reactions

In the first few days after their boundary-setting conversation, Tony stopped speaking to his parents. He kept to himself downstairs during the day and went out with friends at night.

"We weren't surprised," Brad told me. "But it still hurt. I tried not to overreact or take things personally. We didn't try to force him to talk, nor did we contribute to the 'cold war.' We just tried to behave as we normally would in the new reality and give Tony the benefit of the doubt. We kept reminding ourselves that we're working on our long game, a healthier relationship down the road, and concentrated on not making things worse in the meantime."

Brad and Tony crossed paths in the kitchen a couple of times during that first week after the conversation. Each time, Brad made a warm overture toward a safe and trust-building conversation, which went something like this:

Brad: Good morning.

Tony: Hmmph.

Brad: What are you up to today?

Tony: Probably looking for a place to live.

Brad: Well, if there's some way that I can help you with anything, just let me know.

Tony: You can start by not kicking me out into the cold.

Brad: I'm sad that this is the message you took from our conversation. We don't want to kick you out. We're just establishing some reasonable ground rules so we can coexist well.

Tony: Well, if you really want to help, you can start by getting rid of the ground rules.

Brad: Sorry, but your mom and I really believe that these boundaries are fair, and will actually help strengthen our relationship by making it easier for us to get along.

Tony: The boundaries are only set on me! What are *you* doing to help us coexist?

Brad: Fair question. We're providing a safe, warm place for you to live for free up until May 1, and after that, for not much money. We're allowing our basement to be open to your friends all day and up to 10:00 p.m. And we're continuing to provide for many of your physical needs and expenses.

Tony: It still doesn't feel right. You're treating me like a kid! I'm almost twenty-nine!

Brad: I actually think we're treating you like a grown-up. I know this is hard. I want us to get through this together. If there's something I can do besides changing the boundaries, I would really love to help.

Tony: No, thanks. Won't be necessary.

These conversations didn't produce any glowing results on the surface, but when Brad relayed them to me, I was still impressed. "Sounds like you did a great job of staying calm, not letting Tony hook you into a fight, and not overreacting to his negative response to the new boundaries."

"Thanks," Brad said. "I tried not to be apologetic about the boundaries themselves, while trying to build relational trust and hope at the same time. It's tricky! Wish I had these skills when I was raising the kids."

"I wish the same thing myself," I said. "The overtures you're making toward Tony will really help him overcome the distorted stories he's likely been telling himself over this hard season."

"What sort of distorted stories?"

"When we experience rejection or significant loss, it's easy to believe little lies about ourselves that aren't true," I said. "In Tony's case, they might sound like, 'I'm not lovable. Even my parents don't love me.' 'I'm just a loser.' 'My parents don't want me around.' 'There's no hope for me.' 'I must be so terrible that even my parents are rejecting me.' 'My parents are the problem.' 'My parents are bad,' and so on and so forth."

"Whoa, is all that really swirling around in his head?"

"I don't know. I'm just trying to give you a snapshot of how people in his situation might respond."

3. Empathize with, but Don't Assume Ownership of, Their Feelings

One afternoon in the early days after the conversation, Brad and Tony crossed paths in the garage. Here's a look at their brief exchange:

Brad: Hey, Tony.

Tony: Hmmph.

Brad: How are you?

Tony: Depressed, frankly. Hopeless. My girlfriend rejected me. My work rejected me. Now my parents are rejecting me and kicking me out. But thanks for asking! And how are *you*?

Brad: I'm sad that you're so sad, son. I know this is a really hard season. I'm still hoping that you'll choose to stay here, because your mom and I really want to help you through this. But if you choose to move out, just know that we love you very much, and our door will always be open to you, under the new arrangement.

Brad did four clever things in this conversation:

1. He didn't minimize how difficult and sad this was for Tony. He offered sincere empathy.
2. He didn't get into another argument with Tony about whether or not he was getting "thrown out."
3. He didn't soften or renegotiate the boundaries.
4. He expressed his love for Tony clearly and reiterated his desire to help him.

Brad relayed this interaction to me during our next phone call, and I was impressed. This was a major victory. "In the past when Tony made self-pitying comments like these, how would you have responded?" I asked.

"Well, I'd feel overwhelmed and take on Tony's problem as my own," he said. "This time was different. My heart was still breaking for the guy during the conversation, but even as we were talking, I could recognize that the pain Tony is experiencing is from consequences of his own choices—and it's no longer my job to own or remove those consequences. I'm the owner of my own sadness over the relational gap between us, and my support system is helping me deal with that. Tony needs to learn to deal with his own sadness too."

Brad and Barb reiterated their offer to pay for Tony to seek counseling with a therapist of his choice. He still turned them down, but with less vigor than before.

Eventually Brad noticed Tony was softening. About two weeks after the conversation, Tony came upstairs around 7:00 a.m. as Brad and Barb were having breakfast and poured himself a cup of coffee. He seemed calmer but still looked hurt, and a little embarrassed. He was an insightful young man, and no doubt he was cringing a bit as he reflected on the things he'd said to his parents during that difficult conversation.

"Wanna join us?" Brad asked.

"Sure," said Tony, sitting down at the kitchen table. "Look, uh,

I'd like to try to make these new ground rules of yours work. I know I reacted pretty awfully when you first brought them up, but I've had some time to think. I'm not loving them, and the noise one seems a little uptight. But this is your home, and I can't say they're unfair expectations."

Barb's eyes filled, and Brad reached over and hugged his son. "Glad to hear it, Tony. Thanks."

"I have several job interviews lined up for the next two weeks," he continued, "and I've got a couple more leads to follow up on too. I need to buy some new clothes for those interviews, and I'm wondering if you'd consider renegotiating some of the details of the boundaries."

"What do you have in mind?" Brad asked.

"Could we postpone the first rent date from May 1 to June 1? The new clothes will set me back a bit, and if I land one of these jobs, it will be a while before I get my first paycheck."

Brad looked at Barb for input. "That seems like a reasonable request," she said. "June 1 it is."

"Thanks," Tony said. "Can I make one more ask? Could you extend the quiet curfew to 11:00 p.m. instead of 10:00 p.m.? Some of my friends don't get off work until 8:00 p.m., so that doesn't give us much time."

"I think this boundary needs to stay put," Brad said. "Let's see how things go between now and June 1. We can renegotiate after that. But remember, if you want to have a party or special event on a particular night, let's talk. We're totally up for making exceptions if we all plan ahead."

"Fair enough," Tony said. "And I won't even ask about lightening up on the bathroom-cleaning boundary!"

He smiled, and so did his parents.

4. Don't Be Swayed by Negative Internal Voices—Stay the Course

Brad and Tony both played familiar roles in the dance that has kept them stuck over the years. Tony played the role of the needy, underperforming child, while Brad played the role of the long-suffering, rescuing parent. Tony had become brilliant at enticing his father into this comfortable dance. And historically, the old negative voices in Brad's mind led him to second-guess any attempt to escape the dance. Some of the phrases Tony used to keep his father in the dance included:

- "What kind of father doesn't want to help his son succeed?"
- "I'm not asking for the moon! I just need a little more time. Don't reject me in my time of need!"
- "My friends can count on their parents in times of need. I wish I could count on you."
- "Just because I'm not perfect like my sisters doesn't mean you need to punish me."

And when Brad was tempted to shift into a more protecting mode and stand up for himself, he'd be plagued by his own inner voices of self-doubt:

- *Am I being too selfish? Controlling?*
- *If I don't bail Tony out now, he'll hate me forever.*
- *What kind of father abandons his son?*
- *A better father would know exactly what to do right now.*
- *If I were a better father, Tony wouldn't be in this situation to begin with.*
- *What will others think if we stop supporting our son?*

Brad had been staying attentive to these defeating voices, and combatting them with more honest, accurate self-talk: "I am reminding myself that the most kind, courageous way I can build my relationship with Tony is to maintain these boundaries and not reenter our old, destructive patterns."

Tony landed a job from one of his interviews, and when June 1 rolled around, he somewhat begrudgingly handed his dad a check for $500. It was a good start. But about a month later, Tony had a movie night with friends in the basement that lasted until nearly midnight. Their efforts at keeping things quiet fell short, and Brad approached Tony the next morning.

"That was your first grace slipup on the 10:00 p.m. noise restriction," he said. "I got woken up at 10:41, 11:29, and 12:24, not that I was taking note."

"Sorry, Dad," Tony said, without attitude or sarcasm. He seemed to be sincerely sorry.

A month later, Tony approached Brad and requested permission to have some friends over the following Saturday to watch a big regional baseball game. "It's an East Coast game," Tony said, "and I'm guessing it might go later than ten central time. For this one night, could we relax the 10:00 p.m. noise curfew?"

Brad was thrilled with the respectful way Tony made the request. He clearly was trying to honor the boundary. "Sure, son," he said. "And thanks for planning ahead."

When he recounted to me this much happier exchange with his son, Brad added, "I was happy to flex, because he was so dang respectful about the whole thing."

"How late do you think they'll keep you up?" I asked.

"Not a minute past ten!" he said. "Barb and I bought earplugs, but don't tell Tony!"

Over time, the cold war between Brad and Tony thawed completely, and their relationship reached a new level of maturity and intimacy. Several months after starting his new job, Tony had saved enough money to rent an apartment of his own. Brad and Barb helped him move in.

When the last box was lugged from the moving van to the new apartment, Tony extended his hand to his dad and said, "I didn't exactly love those boundaries you guys set with me, but looking back, maybe it was the kick in the butt I needed to get out of that rut. And,

Dad, you really seem . . . different to me lately, compared to how you used to be. I like it."

"In what way?" Brad asked.

"I mean, you've always been a great dad and all, but, to be honest, I always sensed I could get my way with you if I tried hard enough. No offense."

"None taken. And you're probably right, you could have."

"I like things the way they are now," Tony said. "I feel more certain of you today than I ever did before."

"I like things better now, too, son," Brad said. "I'm more certain of me too."

TWELVE

CONCLUSION

A couple of decades ago, in a moment of misguided overconfidence, I decided I would attempt a do-it-yourself home renovation in a corner of our unfinished basement. All I needed to do was put up some walls with a few electrical outlets, run some speaker wire behind those walls, hang a door, lay some tile, texture the ceiling, install ceiling lights, and then paint the whole room. How hard could it be, right? I skimmed a book or two on remodeling and dove in.

Not long into my renovation, I began running into some unexpected challenges: there was a water pipe right where I wanted a power outlet to go; the existing fuse box didn't have room for any additional fuses; and my pre-hung door wouldn't hang right. Despite the challenges, I persevered, and eventually completed the renovation. Once my family and I were able to enjoy the fruits of my labor, I was glad I had persisted. And I learned two valuable lessons about undertaking the task of renovation:

1. Plan for unexpected challenges.
2. The end result will be worth the effort, even when it's hard.

These lessons ring true for renovating our relationships as well.

Both personally and professionally, I've found that when life is difficult, some sort of relational disappointment lies at the root of the problem. As we've covered in this book, when relational disappointment strikes, we must first right-size the gap so we're managing the real issue. Unexpected challenges often show up when we try to clarify the gap, because we may not like the answers to the questions we must ask ourselves.

Sometimes when we ask ourselves, What do I *really* want? we recognize that we have desires or expectations that aren't realistic, and likely cannot be met. Therefore, instead of demanding the other person meet those unrealistic expectations and becoming resentful when they cannot, we simply need to grieve what is not to be, and then choose more reasonable expectations.

Similarly, when we ask ourselves, What's *really* going on? we may find it uncomfortable to realize that we've distorted reality through self-deception. Perhaps we've portrayed the other person as worse than they really are (we accuse), or we've portrayed ourselves as better than we really are (we excuse). Or maybe we're making the problem less significant than it really is (we minimize), or we're lessening our own responsibility for the situation (we rationalize).

These unexpected challenges require courage and perseverance. If you find yourself tempted to accuse/excuse or minimize/rationalize, take heart. You're normal. And by saying no to self-deception and yes to right-sizing the gap with honesty and humility, you'll significantly increase your satisfaction in all your relationships.

Sometimes, even when we know what we *should* do, whether that means building more bridges or setting more boundaries, we struggle to actually *do* the right thing. It is human nature to exaggerate the cost of initiating change and to minimize the benefits.

In renovating relationships, resisting change plays out in two ways:

1. If we're prone toward over-protecting but more accepting is needed, we're tempted to stop short of doing what we know we should do. We tell ourselves that the other person will take advantage of us unless we protest and make a big deal about

things. Or we convince ourselves that it will be a slippery slope if we don't over-protect, that the other person's behavior will only get worse if we let them off the hook.

2. If we're prone toward over-accepting but more protecting is needed, we're tempted to stop short of action by convincing ourselves that the other person will pitch a fit if we set a boundary, and it's just not worth the hassle. So we settle for the status quo.

I can relate to both reactions, having been on both sides of the equation. But making those needed changes is rarely as scary as we fear, while failing to do so means choosing to settle for mediocre or unsatisfying relationships. Following through, even when it's hard, is the only way to bring lasting change to the relationships that matter most. And, in the end, it will be worth it.

If you've applied the lessons from this book to a relational disappointment, then you:

- understand what you *really* want;
- know what's *really* going on; and
- are clear on whether more accepting or more protecting will help you reach an ideal balance.

Whether you need to set new boundaries or build new bridges, the relational healing and life satisfaction you'll gain will be well worth the effort. You've got this. You know what you need to do. It's time to do it. Renovate your relationships with kindness and courage. You'll be so glad you did.

I wish you well.

S.V.

Acknowledgments

The ideas in this book were distilled from thousands of inter-actions and conversations I've had with people I've encountered over the years. And for each one of you, I'm deeply grateful.

Much of the content in this book—and much of my current teaching, writing, coaching, and consulting—has its origin in the workshops that my teammates and I've created to help people build better relationships. These teammates are among the most amazing leaders and friends in my life. Thank you to (in alphabetical order): Lisa Bohn, Leigh Carlson, Katie Franzen, Beki Grissom, Chris Hurta, Deirdré Jansen Van Rensburg, Amy Kranicki, Karis Reichert, Deb Shurtz, and Chrissie Steyn.

Thank you to the early readers of this manuscript who offered fantastic critique, coaching, and feedback. They are (in alphabetical order): Shane Farmer, Scott Gibson, Sue Hood, Sandy McConkey, David Mitchell, Sarah Riebe, and Deb Shurtz.

Deep gratitude to my dear friend, Dr. Andy Hartman, who not only read the manuscript and offered his professional insights, but also regularly encourages and coaches me through all that life brings.

A special word of thanks to the remarkable team at Nelson Books. As a first-time author, I'm grateful for the extra doses of patience and direction provided by Jessica Wong and Sujin Hong. To my agent, Chris Ferebee, I thank you for your wisdom, guidance, and expertise, which led to the publication of this book.

ACKNOWLEDGMENTS

The lion's share of my gratitude goes to my life partner, primary editor, and wife, September, who has read this book, reread it, and then read it again. With each reading, she has offered monumental suggestions, rewrites, and edits. My work and this book would not have been possible without her ability to take another person's ideas and put them into intelligible words.

Notes

Chapter 1

1. Arthur Schopenhauer, *Parerga und Paralipomena*, vol. II (1851; repr., Oxford University Press, 1974), chap. XXXI, sect. 396.
2. Eugene Peterson, foreword to *Embracing Brokenness: How God Refines Us Through Life's Disappointments*, by Alan Nelson (Colorado Springs: NavPress, 2002).
3. Having lived and worked both inside and outside the church, I feel confident that the material in this book applies equally to the religious and the nonreligious alike. We all struggle with setting boundaries and building bridges, and the concepts in this book are rooted in psychology, physiology, and life experience. Regardless of your worldview, I think you'll find these concepts helpful in navigating troubled relationships.

Chapter 2

1. Henry Cloud and John Townsend, *Boundaries: When to Say Yes, How to Say No to Take Control of Your Life* (Grand Rapids: Zondervan, 1992), 107.

Chapter 4

1. Robert Frost, "Mending Wall" (1914), lines 27 and 45.
2. Cloud and Townsend, *Boundaries*, 115.

Chapter 6

1. Kerry Patterson, Joseph Grenny, Ron McMillan, and Al Switzler, *Crucial Conversations: Tools for Talking When Stakes Are High* (New York: McGraw-Hill, 2002).

Chapter 7

1. The Arbinger Institute, *Leadership and Self-Deception: Getting Out of the Box* (Oakland, CA: Berrett-Koehler Publishers, 2000), 68.

2. Much thanks to the Arbinger Institute for their illustration of "How I Started to See Myself" and "How I Started to See Nancy," which served as the framework for this table. *Leadership and Self-Deception: Getting Out of the Box*, 72.

Chapter 8

1. This quote is often erroneously attributed to Abraham Lincoln. You can read the history of this quote at https://quoteinvestigator.com /2014/03/29/sharp-axe/.

Chapter 9

1. John Gottman and Nan Silver, *The Seven Principles for Making Marriage Work* (New York: Random House, 2002), loc. 818–19, Kindle.

Chapter 11

1. Patterson, Grenny, McMillan, and Switzler, *Crucial Conversations*.

ABOUT THE AUTHOR

Scott Vaudrey is a retired emergency department doctor and pastor. He received his MD from the University of Washington in 1988, and MA in transformational leadership from Bethel University in 2005. After transitioning from medicine to ministry, he served as a pastor for sixteen years, helping people navigate their relational challenges. Today he splits his time between executive coaching and speaking to staff teams, businesses, nonprofits, and churches around the country about how to improve relationships and create thriving team cultures.

Scott and his wife, September, live in the northwest suburbs of Chicago. They raised five children and have three grandkids—and counting.